FOREST POWER

Adventures in Ecology and Forest Management

Articles From

The Taos News Natural Resources Notebook
2007 – 2012

Lawrence W. Vincent

Forest BioPower - 2012

ISBN-10: 0615660126

EAN-13: 9780615660127

Library of Congress Control Number: 2012942630

Forest BioPower, San Cristobal, New Mexico

TABLE OF CONTENTS

FROM A POET AND NOVELIST'S PERSPECTIVE:
FORWARD BY RON CHAVEZ*

Is a toothpick a tree? Is the air we breathe a tree? Obviously not, but both come to us thanks to the trees. Forest Power is not a random title chosen by Lawrence (Larry) Vincent. That trees in the forest exert a powerful influence on the life of this planet earth is an indisputable fact.

A toothpick is but a tiny example of the influence of a tree. From this meager item, think wooden bridges, railroad ties, a dining room table, a wood-sided house. Point is you can hardly exist as a human bring without depending on something produced from a tree.

But the most critical of all that trees produce is the air we breathe through photosynthesis. Photosynthesis is an extremely complex process. In its simplest form, this important reaction converts CO_2 [carbon dioxide] and H_2O [water] plus energy [sunlight] into O_2 [oxygen] and $(C_6H_{12}O_6)$ [glucose]. The oxygen goes into the air you breathe.

Now this is forest power, the very thing we require for life itself. What Dr. Vincent has created is a template not only of all that a forest contributes towards the very life of our planet earth, but also what we need to do to preserve it.

In having read Forest Power I was left with a sinking feeling because it made me realize how we humans are violating the natural place forests occupy in the very existence of human life. Yet we ravage them worse than wild fires struck by lightning.

Vincent grew up under the shadow of the forest-wrapped Sangre de Cristo Mountains in northern New Mexico. That he went on to become not only an avid student, but an expert of life in the trees from these mountain-side beginnings, is a blessing for all of us who love the land and life itself for he has left us a legacy in his book Forest Power for all mankind to read and understand the complexity required to preserve our precious forests.

To go out and hug a tree or save the spotted owl can be more harmful than helpful. The heart and soul of forest conservation are detailed extensively and powerfully here in Forest Power by Dr. Vincent. We should instead hug this marvelous book and hold it forever close in the understandings of our mind.

* Taos New Mexico Poet - Route 66 Storyteller

Starting Our Adventure

Venturing into the complex world of forest ecosystems can be quite an experience. This is a "place" where things are often not as they seem on the surface. Simple views are so often misleading when we fail to go into depth on the complex dynamics of forest ecosystems. Something that appears to be horrible can actually be beneficial over time and conversely, a situation that appears good may be detrimental. And time is an essential element in the equation. It's implicit in the term "dynamics". Change over time is a key. Forest ecosystems are constantly changing. Nothing remains the same in the flow of time. Understanding the multiple and interacting relationships among plants and animals, large and small, is not easy. However forming a viewpoint and actions without undertaking this adventure can lead to unintended consequences resulting from stances assumed with the best of intentions but lacking in an adequate understanding of ecology.

Our challenge here, both for the reader and the writer, not to mention the scientists who must take it all apart (virtually) identify, understand the pieces and then put them back together as a system model, is to get a basic comprehension of forest ecosystems for various motives. Wanting to know can be just for the satisfaction of knowing or, for example, to be a better activist in conservation. For our students it could be to decide whether or not to go into ecology, forest management or other related fields, all of which offer great potential for careers with challenging and satisfying employment opportunities. Even the sky is not the limit nowadays. Astrobiology and extraterrestrial ecology are new careers in this age of information and space. The process of finding life forms here on Earth in the harshest, worst, habitats, is being used to study the prospects of life on other celestial bodies. The discovery of an ever-increasing number of planets outside our solar system is literally opening up new worlds. Ecology plays an important role in this adventure.

Of course this is adventure. Even here on earth there is so much that we don't know about our forest and non-forest ecosystems. As is usual in science, every new answer from a discovery leads to multiple new questions. This is a never-ending process and any adventurous soul can get on this "train" at anytime. There will always be plenty to do and great challenges.

The intention of the author is to introduce readers to a world of adventure; admittedly to get the curious and the motivated would-be conservationist hooked on the fascinating fields of ecology and forest management and to discover the power of forests.

Forest management is to be understood in undertaking this adventure as any form of administrating, conserving, taking care of forest ecosystems whether or not it involves extractive processes i.e. timber harvesting of some form, or other extractive activities. In either case preservation or productive management, sustainability is the underlying principle. And sustainability is not just environmental or ecological. It is also economic and socio-political. Just setting aside an area and excluding extractive activities does not guarantee sustainability. Putting too much forest area under extractive, productive use most likely is not sustainable (nor is it possible due to specific topographic and geologic conditions). Likewise, putting too much forest area under preservation is also unsustainable, either economically or socio-politically. True sustainability lies in achieving a balance between the two.

Balance is the key to satisfaction and sustainability; combining the terms we could refer to "sustainable satisfaction" of society. In this case balance between sustainable non-extractive forest management (SNEFM) and sustainable productive forest management (SPFM) should appear to be an obvious strategy in our public and private forests. The actual degree of balance, a ratio of, say 70-30 or 60-40, will probably be different between public and private forestry and will also depend on topography, soils and forest stand conditions.

The general public is interested in our forest resources and concerned about them. Many want to help in their conservation through some form of activism. Our public forests include a wide range of ecosystems in the west from grasslands and meadows to old-growth mixed conifers. In between we find brush chaparrals sparse low forests such as pinyon-juniper and ponderosa pine stands, the latter ranging from park-like open stands to fairly dense older growth forests and thick young "dog hair" stands. Interspersed in the mixed conifers we find aspen stands that are especially visible in the fall.

Widespread interest and multiple cases of involvement of environmental activists who often are not adequately oriented due to lack of basic knowledge of ecology, have been the reason for indulging in writing material designed for the general public. In 2007 The Taos News had the vision of undertaking the publishing of these ideas in the Natural Resources Notebook bi-weekly column.

Before jumping in to the adventure, now all in one place instead of the necessarily short articles, we'll briefly go into the history of the Natural Resources Notebook.

Where "Forest Power" came from

The first article of The Taos News (Taos, New Mexico, USA) Natural Resources Notebook "<u>Global warming and forest health</u>" was published in the Oct 18 – 24, 2007 edition. The editor at that time was Gerald Garner Jr. who coined the name of the column and set up the bi-weekly routine. It followed separate articles published in the My Turn section, which led to the idea of a column. The fourth anniversary (October, 2011) seemed to be an opportunity to make the whole collection available to Taos News readers and extend beyond to a wider audience. As work continued on this book in late 2011 and early 2012 additional articles were included. "Forest Power: Adventures in Ecology and Forest Management" includes 99 articles published in the Natural Resources Notebook series. A list of the articles in chronological order is included in Appendix A.

The Taos News writing effort has been voluntary, motivated by a desire to share ideas, experiences and viewpoints with readers *aqui en Taos* and beyond through the fine Internet access provided by The Taos News and other internet media. The author has not received payment from any organization nor person for the column. Most of the manuscripts, as sent to the editor, have been available on the author's website where the material where they are available free of charge. Now they are available in this book in a package, organized in a logical topic-by-topic order with comments.

Introduction to the basic ecological foundations of our adventures

Forest ecosystems are dynamic things. They are constantly changing, usually slowly, inconspicuously but sometimes drastically due to fire or other agents, either natural or human. Understanding their ecology is fundamental to any sort of activism or to just plain fulfill the desire to know. The interactions among the different parts of forest ecosystems are complex. Understanding them requires a certain degree of thinking along a systems approach where the whole is broken down into its parts, its components, and analyzed to determine how each is related to others. The sum of all these interactions and relationships, such as competition, defines how the system as a whole will respond to outside influences. "Outside" means that system boundaries have been defined. For a forest ecosystem, outside factors include, for example, climate and human actions. How does a prolonged drought affect a pinyon-juniper or ponderosa forest? One notable thing is an outbreak of western pine beetle or bark beetle. Fire, stemming from the beetle event, weather and fuel conditions, is a dramatic event. Some refer to it as nature's pressing the reset button (a term used in a Park Service Bulletin) that starts a whole new set of changes referred to as ecological succession.

The ecology of forest ecosystems: change and resilience

How might we benefit from forest ecosystems' way of being (behavior) in actual and potential ability to change? Growth is a form of positive change. It is a gradual kind of change and is stimulated by apparently

---

negative much more abrupt change i.e. loss of trees and entire stands to fire, insect and disease or by planned or unplanned human actions that reduce forest stand density and thus promote growth.

Forest ecosystems: their potential in a renewable energy strategy

Our national forest resources can play a significant role in over all economic growth and especially in the area of global climate change mitigation and renewable energy. Our huge "green machine" is a remarkable thing. How could we come up with a better mechanism or technology than something that produces energy through growth while at the same time taking carbon dioxide (CO_2), the major greenhouse gas, out of the atmosphere, putting oxygen into it, creating and maintaining jobs and economic opportunities for business of all sizes, generating revenue and, furthermore, supplying natural green-certified wood products? The best part of it is that it runs on solar energy and that it is already in place, more than shovel ready if we figure out how to do it. And, furthermore, it includes storage capacity in the form plant tissues. First of all we have to recognize that it's there and that it can be used in a sustainable manner; and on that basis be willing to make the decisions to try it out, to put it in place at least on an experimental pilot scale. Photosynthesis is a powerful thing. "Green" is chloroplasts in leaves: those tiny elements in leaves that run on solar energy.

**Forest growth and the power of photosynthesis:
Forest Power**

PRESENTATION

The reader will find that the order or presentation of the articles is by topic. A chronological list of articles can be found in Appendix A.

All articles were published in The Taos News Natural Resources Notebook column. The article text, set apart by a different format from other text, is included as sent to the editor, not necessarily as published, though in general very few changes were made. When the published title is different from the article title that appears as a heading, the published title is included in the reference at the beginning of each article. Otherwise only the edition dates and page numbers are provided. In some cases the page number is not available.

The reader will note that the main headings are the topics under which the articles are grouped, while the secondary headings (subtitles) are the article titles themselves, as can be seen in the Table of Contents.

We start with ecology basics. Any form of forest management, meaning for whatever objective the forest owners, the general public in the case of or national forests, must be based on sound ecological principles. For many readers even the origin of the word ecology may be new. From the basics we go on to elemental notions of ecological succession, shade tolerance and forest stand terminology; and then on to forest management and its relation to ecology and forest ecology. The role of forest ecosystem dynamics, especially resilience in response to external events, is a central theme and provides the principles on which forest treatment is based. Treatment can be seen in terms of conservation, in terms of production (wood products and energy), climate change mitigation or any combination of them, as well as other environmental services such as water, clean air, atmospheric carbon balance (or imbalance) recreation, basic science and just plain conservation.

ECOLOGY BASICS

We start with the most elemental consideration of ecology as a science, an endeavor, an interest to pursue and as a basis for knowing what to do or not to do with our forest ecosystem resources.

What is ecology?

The Taos News – Natural Resources Notebook. Nov 15 - 21, 2007. p. B11

Is an ecologist an environmentalist or conversely is an environmentalist an ecologist?

Ecology can be defined in general terms as the study of the relationship of living things with their habitat, which can be thought of as a "house". Actually, the term "ecology" comes from the Greek word "oikos" meaning house; the "ology" part comes from "logies" which means study. Ecology, then, is the study of a "house" and its relationship with a living thing or a community of living things. The "living thing" can be a relatively simple entity such as an animal species. For example we can think of the ecology of the black bear in the Kit Carson Forest and its "house" i.e., its surroundings or habitat. An ecologist will study how the bear relates to its habitat (its environment). Questions that an ecologist will ask are, for example: How much territory does a bear or a bear family require for survival (in other words, how big is its house)? How does its size relate to various elements such as food supply, which in turn depends on vegetation types and soils among many other things?

The living "thing" can be far more complex as, for instance, a forest. In this case we are considering a multitude of different living things, both plant and animal, that live together in a community in a "house" made up of other living things and the physical and climatological habitat in which they exist. Our house, in this case the forest, is also influenced by outside factors such as people who can shape and change the house. There are many relationships among the components of this ecosystem probably the most important of which is competition for food (which in the case of plants includes sunlight - solar energy- and soil nutrients to produce food), water and space. The combination of all of these elements (living and nonliving) can be described as an ecosystem.

Now, let's get really complex and define the "living thing" as human population. Our "house" is the planet Earth. Human ecology therefore is how we relate to our "house" and what we do to it in our attempt to survive and prosper. How we take care of our Earth (how we manage it) is the complex field that we can call "environmental management" which uses ecology and other sciences, technology, economics and politics to apply the knowledge provided by science to a specific problem such as global climate change. The application is the responsibility of those in charge of managing our "house" which include policy makers, resource managers and monitors, all of whom support their actions with scientific knowledge (or at least they should!).

Would it be fair to say that an ecologist is a scientist and that an environmentalist is an activist mostly involved in helping shape policy and independently monitor processes? If the answer is yes, we must be certain that the activists have a sound knowledge of ecology in order to be effective in their actions towards improving the way we treat our "house".

Once again, communication is the key in the management of our environment. In order to preserve, protect, and enrich our ecosystem, our "house," we need to improve communication between the scientific community, the managers of our environment, the environmentalist watchdog organizations, and the general populace.

Again, special thanks to Debbie Ragland, UNM-Taos Geology, for her valuable contribution in reviewing and editing.

The next logical step in our brief consideration of ecology basics, is putting things together in a systems approach: Hence ecosystems.

What is an ecosystem?

<u>What is an Ecosystem? Look around you.</u> *The Taos News – Natural Resources Notebook. March 20 - 26, 2008. p. B13*

An area of sagebrush, such as we see between Las Colonias and Arroyo Hondo, an area of piñon-juniper forest so common in our area or a section of a mountain stream are examples of ecosystems.

The term ecosystem that we so frequently use is a combination of "ecology" or "ecological" and "system". We have already defined ecology in previous articles ("eco" from oikos, which means house or household, and "ology" from logies, which means study) and we defined ecology as the study of the relationship of living organisms (usually fairly complex communities) with their environment (their house). So the "eco" part of ecosystem has to do with ecology or more precisely ecological. The "system" part would appear to be quite clear. However, we often misuse the term, as in someone has a good system of organizing things (should be scheme or method). So, we should define the system part of ecosystem in more formal, scientific terms. A system is an entity either real or abstract made up of elements (components, parts) that are related so as to interact with each other to define a pattern of behaviour, such as response to external stimuli. Something is done to a system and it reacts in a certain way. Let's consider some examples: a computer, an office or a company, a car (or electrical subsystem), a pond (this is the classic example of a simple ecosystem), a forest, the earth as a whole, or the solar system. Therefore, the parts that define a system are: an entity, elements, interrelations among elements, behavior, boundaries, inputs and outputs (that depend upon boundaries). The implication is that a system is dynamic, i.e., it changes over time and responds to external factors in a given way (behavior). Also, it is often complex. So we have characteristics of a system: it is an entity, a "being"; it has a number of elements (parts of a whole) that are related and interact with each other in ways that define a pattern of behavior; and finally, a system has a defined boundary that determines its size and confinement (what is in it and what is not).

We note that behavior is an important aspect in considering an ecosystem. It involves the dynamics and, as an end result, how it reacts to what we do to it or what nature does to it. This is where the implication of management, which involves manipulation of an ecosystem, such as a unit of forest, can be appreciated.

So an ecosystem is an entity, usually a natural system, which is made up of a living community and its environment which can be defined in terms of boundaries. It can be small, like a pond, or huge like our Planet Earth. Around our area we can identify and define some examples of ecosystems. As explained in the opening paragraph, examples of ecosystems in our area could be a sagebrush area such as we see between Las Colonias and Arroyo Hondo or an area of piñon-juniper forest so common in northern

New Mexico. Because an ecosystem has boundaries, we should identify a specific region where the ecosystem exists. This facilitates our description of it and, as we become more serious about our investigations, our study of the ecosystem. So, a lot of what composes an ecosystem depends on how we wish to define it in terms of setting boundaries, either very specific boundaries or more abstract boundaries of an ecosystem (e.g., any sagebrush area, piñon-juniper area or mountain stream).

We'll briefly introduce a related term, "systems ecology". This is the discipline that studies an entity in relation to its ecosystem through use of mathematical, computer and sometimes physical models that help understand them and how an entity responds to stimuli (i.e., the study of its behavior). The idea behind systems ecology is that a complex entity such as an ecosystem can be simplified and represented by a model which describes the dynamics under a given set of conditions and responses to changes in those conditions. These modeling studies can be used to predict outcomes of different alterations (such as management treatments or fire) without actually affecting the real system. It is a sort of laboratory experiment, generally done on a computer, in which we seek answers to the question: "What if ...?" What if we drain a pond? What if there is a fire in a forest stand? What if we harvest timber at a given intensity on a specific area of forest?

What if we continue to put excessive amounts of greenhouse gasses into our atmosphere? Now there's a huge, complex problem where the Earth's biosphere is the system (global warming)!

Again, special thanks to Debbie Ragland, UNM-Taos Geology, for her valuable contribution in reviewing and editing.

As we move on in the basics of ecology, we get to how trees and other plants interact with each other in an ecosystem. Competition is the most important and defining interaction in a forest ecosystem. It largely defines the dynamics.

Competition: A driving force in ecology

The Taos News – Natural Resources Notebook. April 3 - 9, 2008

Would you believe that a tree species cooperates with ants to compete in a tropical forest? There is competition and cooperation in nature, but competition stands out as a major driving force in the relationships among plants and animals in natural and man-made ecosystems.

Plants and animals compete for resources such as food, water and even simply for living space. Anybody who has done gardening knows that you plant carrots rather densely to be sure to have a row, but later you have to thin them out or you don't get any carrots. The baby carrot plants compete with each other more and more as they grow. Some get crowded out naturally. What is happening is competition among individuals. This is an example of intra-specific competition, i.e. competition among individuals of the same species (carrots). In natural plant communities, such as a piñon-juniper forest, there is both intra-specific and inter-specific competition. The latter is competition among individuals of different species. For instance, because they're taller than other plants, the trees get to have the first crack at sunlight, which is a major resource (energy). Smaller plants under the trees have to find a way to compete. They are at a disadvantage (size is pretty important, especially height). Over long periods of time, competitive strategies are developed through natural selection: the survival of the fittest. As a result, some species have acquired the ability to withstand (tolerate) shade. This gives them an advantage in their situation of disadvantage, being smaller and over-shaded by the trees. Others plants have developed means of "finding" open spots in which they can grow. This strategy involves having abundant, lightweight seeds that can be carried by wind. A very small percentage of the seeds actually land in open places where they can germinate and grow (and a smaller number yet grow to maturity). This strategy involves sheer numbers: If you are a plant and you're weak or have a disadvantage, you survive as a species by having large numbers of offspring with very low survival rates. This is sort of a "shotgun approach" to find a place where you can compete.

A major factor in the outcome of competition is the environment or habitat in which it takes places. How big is the "house"? (from the definition of ecology: oikos refers to house.) Or, how capable is the "house" of supporting plants and animals? This is the carrying capacity of a given site. A given physical place, which means a specific area with its topography (slope and exposure), soil and climate (average sunlight, wind and availability of water) will have a certain amount of resources for a plant community. Think of an ecosystem made up of a given physical place and a plant-animal community. This could be a specific area of our *piñon*-juniper forest example. This, put in terms of economics, is the principle of limited resources. A given site has limited energy (sunlight), water, space and nutrient resources. Plants and animals that live on this site have to compete for these resources in order to survive. They will grow in size and numbers until they reach the carrying capacity. After that, theoretically there will be no net growth, only growth to replace individuals that die.

Back to competitive strategies: plants and animals have developed a wide range of them through natural selection under sometimes fierce competitive pressure. Some of these involve chemical "warfare". The skunk comes to mind. Plants also use chemicals in what is called allelopathy. Certain plants can excrete chemicals that inhibit the establishment (germination of seeds) and growth of other plants in their immediate vicinity. Many mammal and bird species use territoriality to compete. A truly admirable strategy is symbiosis between two different species that cooperate to be better competitors. In tropical forests in western Venezuela and the Amazon basin, a tree species, Triplaris sp. vara santa (due to its showy flowers) or palo María (Venezuela)and palo diablo (Bolivia), lives in association with a species of ants. The tree provides living quarters while the ants provide protection from other plants (vines and weeds) and from animals, including foresters who are trying to do their job and accidentally lean on one of these trees. That only happens once to a given forester. The ant bite includes a toxic chemical that causes quite a rash and pain. Competition is the driving force. It was what resulted in the symbiotic relationship that gave them advantages in competing with other plants and animals.

Competition in ecosystems leads to efficiency, specialization, adaptation and diversification of living things.

Again, special thanks to Debbie Ragland, UNM-Taos Geology, for her valuable contribution in reviewing and editing.

Logically, we would assume that as the forest gets thicker there will be more competition. Following the reasoning, at some point available soil moisture and other resources, including just plain physical space, will be taken up. This is the theoretical ecological threshold where there will be no more net growth. This upper limit of forest biomass is the carrying capacity. Our next matter to consider is the idea of carrying capacity as a limit.

Carrying capacity in ecology

The Taos News – Natural Resources Notebook. June 19-25, 2008. p. B10

How much is enough? How much is too much in an ecosystem? How much of what? The answers are related to biomass and carrying capacity.

An ecosystem is made up of a physical environment (the physical inorganic, non-living component) and a more or less complex association of living things, the biotic component. The physical environment or habitat, the house (do you remember oikos meaning house or household in the origin of the term ecology?) is mainly climate, soil and topography, which in complex interactions provide the resources for the living component. The resources are sunlight (solar energy), water (atmospheric and soil moisture), carbon dioxide, mineral nutrients and just plain living space. As we have seen, living beings, both plant and animal compete for these resources (our reference to "Competition: a Driving Force in Ecology" The Taos News, April 13, 2008 – available on the Taos News website). Let's consider an ecosystem that is on a specific site, a physical location. (The site is part of the ecosystem), which can be poor in resources or rich. Think of a desert or arctic tundra in comparison with a lush Tennessee valley, a high mountain meadow in our area or a humid tropical forest. It is obvious that a lush site, having more moisture, warmth and nutrients will be able to support a greater total biomass (total amount of all living things) than the "poorer", harsher desert or arctic tundra. What we are referring to as "poor" or "rich" has to do with carrying capacity. The question is: How much biomass can a given site sustain? What do we mean by biomass? Basically it is the total amount of living organisms, both plant and animal, large and small, even microscopic. We can think of the total weight of all living things on a unit of site, usually expressed in per acre basis (or metric: per hectare. As a refresher, remember that weight is the interaction between mass of an object and the Earth's gravity. Mass is constant whether here in Taos or on the Moon or Mars. An object's weight will be quite different on the Moon or Mars due to less gravity. Since for the time being we're limited to Earth's ecosystems, biomass is simply the total weight of all living things.

Carrying capacity, therefore, is the upper limit of the amount of living things that a given site (as part of the ecosystem that we are interested in) is capable of sustaining. We can think of it as a theoretic reference point at which net growth stops in an ecosystem. Any growth that takes place is to replace organisms that die or are consumed by other critters. In forest management, carrying capacity is an important reference point, which can guide us in our attempts to achieve our goals, especially regarding timber production. If we try to keep our forest too close to carrying capacity, competition will be too severe and as a result we will lose growth and probably also have an unhealthy forest. If we thin so heavily that we are too far below carrying capacity, we will be sacrificing production or simply have a forest that is too open. Note that "too open" is largely dependent on our management objectives. If cattle grazing is an objective "too open" for timber production may be good. It means that we are more interested in grass (which needs more sunlight) for meat than timber.

In manmade ecosystems as for example a cornfield, carrying capacity can be increased through cultivation techniques, such as using fertilizers and irrigating. The soil can also be modified to a certain extent through plowing and disking which modify soil structure (making it looser). Carrying capacity in natural ecosystems can also be positively modified to a limited extent. In negative terms they can be severely modified through mismanagement and even overt intentional destruction.

Let's consider the carrying capacity of our total ecosystem: the biosphere of our Planet Earth. How many human beings and other organisms can it support? That will depend on how we manage it and also how we manage ourselves (war or peace?), considering resource allocation in the present environment of globalization. The bottom line is sustainability.

One of the most striking forms of competition in forest ecosystems is visible above ground. It's for sunlight. The carrying capacity threshold will vary depending on how the tree species in the ecosystem are able to cope with shade. Obviously as a forest gets thicker there is more shade. Trees compete to be in the upper canopy where more sunlight is available. In the tropics, some trees even climb onto other trees to get sunlight (example: *Ficus* spp.). A tree species' ability to cope is referred to as shade tolerance. Shade tolerance can be thought of as an adaptation to conditions in forests. Being able to survive under the shade of other trees has its advantages. So this leads us to our next topic in which we will also introduce the concept of forest stand and age distribution.

SHADE TOLERANCE, UNEVEN-AGED AND EVEN-AGED STANDS

Shade tolerance in forest ecology and management

The Taos News – Natural Resources Notebook. June 25 – July 1, 2009. p. B11

Is shade good or bad for trees?

A major factor in explaining the ecology of even-aged and uneven-aged forest stands (previous article) is shade tolerance. Trees and tree species can be classified according to the degree to which they can tolerate shade. The fact that trees tolerate shade does not mean that they prefer shade. Trees like most plants depend on the sun for their energy in contrast to animals that get their energy indirectly through food. So very few plants actually like shade. Trees get radiation energy directly from the sun, while we get chemical energy indirectly by way of plants' photochemical process (photosynthesis) that converts atmospheric Carbon dioxide into carbohydrates, which are food for animals and people.

Shade is not a good thing for primary producers: green plants. However, a little shade can be a good thing. Even though trees generally prefer full sunlight, under dry conditions, meaning the combination of climate and soil, some degree of shade may well mean perishing or surviving: there is an interaction between shade tolerance and habitat conditions. Put in a different way, a tree that does not tolerate shade in a moist soil may actually need shade in a dryer soil. Trees growing in a good soil (it can provide sufficient moisture) can tolerate more exposure to the drying effects of high temperatures, low humidity and wind. In other words, a little shade is good to protect from drying in a soil that cannot provide sufficient moisture. The ability to do well in the shade is a competitive advantage, which means that shade-tolerant species will eventually replace intolerants.

Even-aged forest stands are made up mostly of shade intolerant species. In contrast, uneven-aged stands are mostly made up of shade-tolerants. Consider some of our local tree species and forest stands. Aspen is typically shade-intolerant, which means that it doesn't regenerate under its own shade and therefore tends to be even-aged. We can observe mature looking aspen stands in which the understory is made up mostly of spruce and fir. The latter are gradually replacing the aspen in a process called ecological succession. Spruce and fir are generally considered shade-tolerants, which in this case is to their advantage in taking over the aspen stands. They can regenerate and grow in the shade of the aspen.

Our pinyon-juniper or "PJ" are a typical association or forest type. Are they even-aged or uneven-aged stands? There is no easy answer. They seem to be a stable community meaning that without fire, bark beetle or human events, their species composition essentially remains the same over time. At least they do not appear to be in the process of being replaced, as is the case of aspen. Also P-Js live in dryer habitats which limit the potential for their replacement by truly shade tolerants.

Shade tolerance is decisive in prescribing forest treatment. If we're dealing with shade-intolerants, we can't expect them to regenerate and grow under the forest canopy. They need full sunlight. Consequently, we (or nature) must create adequate conditions. No shade means no trees, which in the end means clear-cutting or at least very heavy thinning. Conversely, in dealing with shade-tolerants we (or nature) don't have to make open spaces. The prescription in this case will be selection cutting. Clear-cutting and selection cutting are silvicultural systems, again, keeping in mind a balance between preserved and productive forests.

Shade tolerance is a key factor in considering a two-category classification of forests regarding age distribution: Uneven-aged and even-aged stands.

Uneven-aged forest stands: Part 1

The Taos News – Natural Resources Notebook. July 9 - 15, 2009

In prescribing a forest treatment, or determining if such is needed, we need to find out what kind of forest stand we have. In the last article, we referred to two types of forest (even-aged and uneven-aged) largely in relation to shade tolerance.

A stand is a sort of abstract, hypothetical area of forest that is mostly uniform in characteristics and each stand is different from another. That is why treatment should be prescribed for a specific stand. A forest stand can also be a physical "place" that corresponds to the abstract entity. One way to look at it is to consider a forest type, like, for example our pinyon-juniper ("P-J") forests. A stand would be a set of conditions within the P-J forest. It would most likely be related to density (number of trees/acre). It also could be a variant based on the relative proportions of pinyon and juniper trees or on soil conditions.

So, what is an uneven-aged stand? As the term implies it's a forest stand in which a range of ages and sizes of trees are present. A further implication is that it is a relatively stable forest, meaning that the over all species composition remains generally the same over time. All forest are constantly changing, but we can think of two general types of change: 1) relatively slow constant change that takes place through growth and regeneration in which the species regenerated are the same as those that make up the canopy; and 2) a transformational change in which one forest community is gradually replaced by a different community. An example of the latter is a mature aspen stand (aspen makes up the canopy) under which spruces and firs are getting established and slowly growing. This natural process of replacement is ecological succession. The spruces and firs tolerate shade; that is they can regenerate (be born), survive and grow in the shade of the canopy, although they do not like shade. They are referred to as shade-tolerant. Eventually the mature, senile, aspen die off leaving a new spruce fir community or stand. As a result a beautiful aspen stand is replaced by a no-less-beautiful spruce-fir stand in Nature's process of constant renewal. Nature does not like things to remain the same.

The relatively slow constant change that takes place through growth and regeneration in which the species regenerated are the same as those that make up the canopy characterizes an uneven-aged stand. In our spruce fir stands, change is taking place through a constant process of regeneration (of spruces and firs) under the spruce-fir canopy, mortality and growth. Mortality refers to the fact that not all newborn trees survive. In fact most of them don't. Trees in a forest are in an intensive process of competition for resources, mainly energy and water, but also for physical space and soil nutrients.

In uneven-aged stands that are deemed too thick, the most likely treatment is a form of selection cutting, which involves removal of some mature trees (timber harvesting, logging) and some thinning of smaller trees. Here diameter distribution is an important variable, which can be used to balance the tree removal process in silvicultural treatment. This is referred to as a selection system in the context of sustainable forest management.

Again, we should consider maintaining a balance between forest management for preservation and production.

Uneven-aged stands: Part 2

The Taos News – Natural Resources Notebook. July 23 - 29, 2009

If uneven-aged stands tend to regenerate maintaining a fairly similar age/size structure and species composition, then are they perpetual? Do they remain the same "forever"? Nothing in nature remains the same forever; mountains and ecosystems change, the former very slowly over geologic time, the latter over a shorter timescale.

Being made up mostly of shade-tolerant tree species, uneven-aged stands tend to be more stable than even-aged stands. The latter are made up mostly of shade intolerant tree species such as our aspen and tend to be gradually replaced in ecological succession by shade-tolerants such as spruces and firs. Until fairly recently, forest ecologists referred to the spruce-fir uneven-aged stands as representing a climax stage in ecological succession meaning that the ecosystem has reached situation where it is stable, in equilibrium with the combination climate and soil (the habitat component of an ecosystem). This would tend to suggest that no further change occurs unless there is a major event such as fire, widespread disease or a heavy insect infestation. In reality, changes take place even without such events. One element of gradual change is where natural gaps occur in the forest through natural death of individual trees that fall over and take other trees with them. The gaps often are "filled" with shade intolerants, which can out-grow the shade tolerants. This is referred to as "gap dynamics" and can be considered a sort of "mini ecological succession". It takes place on a small scale determined by the size of the gap. The gap dynamics phenomenon is quite visible in tropical forests as well as our own temperate forests, only in the tropics the pace is greater; gaps are created and filled at a faster rate due to the more favorable habitat conditions of tropical forest ecosystems, mainly temperature and moisture (not having a frozen non-growth season helps a lot).

So uneven-aged stands do change over time and are not truly "climacic", unless the term climax is understood in the context of a dynamic equilibrium. Greater stability means that uneven-aged forests are easier to manage, whether it's for preservation of production. If we're managing for preservation, meaning the forest is under some form of administrative regime, which is necessary for its protection, mainly from human intervention, then greater stability is an advantage (over even-aged stands). However the fact that growth constantly continues resulting the forest getting thicker and thicker means that conditions are gradually being created for the forest to face some sort of abrupt change.

Our uneven-aged forests are also easier to manage for production. Individual mature trees can be removed under what is called a "selection system". Relatively small gaps are created while at the same time forest density (thickness) is regulated to keep the forest healthy. The resulting lack of excessive woody biomass build-up tends to make the forest more stable (less susceptible to abrupt change). Voila, here's an argument in favor of a certain degree of timber removal to in fact improve stability and thus enhance preservation. The key is regulating the amount removed and doing it in such a way as not to damage the environment, mainly the soil. It can be done and needs to be monitored, not only by forest managers but also by the general public through organizations that can hire their own specialists and act as watchdog groups.

Even-aged stands

Even-Aged stands: What are (sic) their future? *The Taos News – Natural Resources Notebook. Aug 6 -12, 2009. p. B12*

What is an even-aged forest stand? Can it be considered a permanent entity or a transition stage? Our aspen stands are probably mostly even-aged. What does this mean for their future?

As the term implies, even-aged stands are ones in which the trees are mostly the same age. This means that they were born pretty much at the same time (obvious!). What's really important is why. Logic would tell us that they must originate from some sort of event that created the conditions for regeneration (being born, surviving and growing) and that the tree species that make up the stand occupy an ecological niche, meaning that they have habitat preferences compatible with the conditions created by that event.

In order for a natural even-aged stand to start, there has to be a "starting point" in which the original forest was removed through fire, widespread blow-down or clearcutting. There also has to be a seed source or other starting material like dormant roots or stumps that sprout. The tree species that occupy the newly opened space to create the even-aged stand generally can't stand shade (they require full sunlight and are referred to as shade intolerants) so they "look for" open spaces. Their competitive advantage over shade tolerants is that they scatter their seeds more effectively and once they establish themselves, they grow faster and dominate the open site.

Even-aged stands can be juvenile, mature or senile. The age of the stand is important in understanding it as well as its origin. A very young stand is quite obvious. It's fairly easy to identify as an even-aged stand. Examples are our aspen, ponderosa pine and dense Gambel (scrub) oak stands. Lodgepole pine is an even better, more evident, example in Colorado in the Pingree Park area west of Fort Collins following bark beetle infestation and fire. It's far more difficult to identify a senile even-aged stand, partly because as it ages it becomes less "even-aged". This happens through the establishment of younger trees of other species under the original even-aged canopy. These new comers to the stand are most likely shade tolerant species that can regenerate under the canopy. They will eventually replace the original even-aged stand, as is the case with spruce and fir replacing aspen. This is an example of ecological succession in which the even-aged stand is a fairly advanced seral stage.

Another stand attribute is the degree of species mixture. Even-aged stands tend to be pure, meaning that they are made up of a single tree species. We would expect this to be related to adaptation to open (highly exposed) conditions. Furthermore, human-made even-aged stands are a common source of pulpwood for paper and cardboard. Forest plantations are a special case of even-aged stands; for example pine plantations for pulpwood in the southeastern United States (slash and loblolly pine) and for combined usage in Eastern Venezuela (Caribbean pine) and Douglas fir in our Pacific Northwest.

So what finally happens to an even-aged stand? It provides the conditions for its own demise. It creates a forest canopy that helps reduce moisture loss (drying) through evapotranspiration thus creating habitat favorable for other tree species, provided that they can tolerate shade. Soil quality, especially as related to moisture providing capacity, is a factor that tends to complicate this seemingly simple process. In very dry soils the process is obscured. This is an example of limiting factors in ecology.

ECOLOGICAL SUCCESSION AND FOREST TREATMENT

Even-aged stands are related to an event. By definition, the fact that all (or most) trees are the same age means that something happened to get them started (regenerated). That something could be and usually is, fire. Clearcutting would be another event. In plantation forestry, tree planting would be the event. Once the event occurs, nature or humans start a recuperation process. In nature it is ecological succession. In forest plantation or tree farming the process is helped along with planting or seeding.

Now we jump into a controversial but key topic in understanding the ecology of forest ecosystems and how productive management practices are based on an understanding of the dynamics involved. To the reader, please keep an open mind and consider it part of our adventure as we delve into clearcutting as an event and as an option in sustainable productive forest management (SPFM).

Clearcutting: Part 1

Clearcutting in the Forest: Part I. *The Taos News – Natural Resources Notebook. Dec 27 2007- Jan 2, 2008*

Would you believe that clearcutting (also written "clear-cutting") which is the total removal of a specific, pre-determined area of forest, is a valid sustainable forest management practice?

The answer lies in an understanding of forest ecology and silviculture, which put briefly is the tending of forests towards given objectives. An internet definition from www.uwsp.edu/natres/nres743/Definitions/Silviculture.htm is given as: "Manipulation of forest vegetation to accomplish a specified set of objectives. It controls forest establishment, composition, and growth". The "silvi" part refers to forest and "culture" to the whole range of regenerating, growing and harvesting practices (like in agriculture). Clearcutting is one of what foresters call "silvicultural systems" which are options that are available in forest management. The choice of an option for a given type of forest and a given management unit depends upon the ecology of the forest, management objectives, economic considerations and public awareness.

First of all let's establish a framework for this discussion. We need to consider a specific case in which we are considering clearcutting: 1. What is the objective: What in the world would we be trying to accomplish? 2. Is it to be in the framework of sustainable management? This means that we are not trying to convert the forest to other uses such as agriculture, urbanization or roads. 3. Why would we, in ecological terms, even consider clearcutting? 4. What is the ecological nature of the tree species that make up the forest community in which we are considering clearcutting? and 5. What is to be the size of each clear-cut unit (each patch of forest)?

In order to address these matters we need to discuss some basic elements of forest ecology and sustainable forest management. Starting with ecology we need to know about the degree of shade tolerance of the tree species we are dealing with. In general we have two extremes: the first is where a species or group of species is able to regenerate and grow in the shade. This means that new seedlings are born (seeds germinated) and can grow under the mature forest canopy. The opposite is where a species or group of species is not able to regenerate and grow in the shade.

In the first case the species is said to be shade tolerant which means it can stand shade but doesn't necessarily like it. The ability to withstand, to tolerate, shade gives the tree species an ecological competitive advantage in maintaining itself in the forest. In other words it has a better chance of survival and prospering in the forest ecosystem. In contrast, a species that cannot withstand shade (they're considered "intolerant") must look elsewhere to establish seedlings (regeneration) in order to maintain itself, to survive and grow and eventually reproduce, passing its genes on to new generations. A shade-intolerant species is at a disadvantage in nature and in order to survive needs to have special characteristics. One of such mechanisms is having light weight seeds, often winged so that they are carried by wind and have a chance of establishing themselves in open areas that may have been created by fire, landslides, wind or by human activities such as clearcutting.

In a forest stand comprised of an intolerant species (such as quaking aspen), once the older mature trees die, they will be replaced by trees belonging to shade-tolerant species (such as spruce and fir). This occurs because the intolerants (aspen) will not have regeneration (young replacement individuals) since new trees cannot establish themselves under the shade of the forest canopy. This phenomenon leads us to consider the concept of ecological succession. We will go into it in Part II of this article, as well as discussing aspects of applying clearcutting in sustainable forest management where one of the main objectives is producing timber. The phrase "one of the main objectives" means that we seldom consider only one use of the forest. In multiple-use (multi-objective) management, restrictions are imposed on one use (such as timber production) in order to make it compatible with other uses (such as water, wildlife and recreation) to achieve sustainability.

The bottom line: Clearcutting is a way to create conditions favorable for shade-intolerant tree species. The answer to the initial question: Yes.

Clearcutting: Part 2

<u>Clearcutting in the Forest: Part II</u>. *The Taos News – Natural Resources Notebook. Jan 3 - 9, 2008*

What does ecological succession have to do with clearcutting?

In part I of this article we covered shade tolerance and related it to clearcutting as an option in sustainable forest management. We will continue to develop the idea in relation to ecological succession. Ecological succession is "The gradual and orderly process of change in an ecosystem brought about by the progressive replacement of one community by another until a stable climax is established" (internet definition from: http://www.thefreedictionary.com/ecological+succession).   A   newly opened up forest stand, often by fire, is "colonized" by light demanding intolerant species. This is an early "seral" stage of succession. As time goes on and the trees grow to close the forest canopy made up of the mature intolerants, shade tolerant species (again spruce and fir) are able to establish themselves and thus constitute the new generation. Eventually, as the intolerants (aspen) complete their life cycle and die off, the young tolerants make up the new forest stand. This is a more advance seral stage of succession. The most advanced stage is referred to as the climax. In our example it is the spruce-fir association which in absence of factors such as fire (or clearcutting) is able to perpetuate itself. The process is more complex. Shade tolerance is not the only factor. We have habitat conditions such as altitude, aspect (direction of exposure:

north or south) and soils to contend with in understanding the process. An example of an even earlier seral stage in natural ecologic succession is when a landslide occurs removing the soil. Now soil must be rebuilt before more advance stages can occur. This is accomplished by colonizers such as lichens and other living forms including minute animals.

Now back to clearcutting. This is done to create conditions favorable to an intolerant species that we want, generally for commercial uses. Because of its inability to tolerate shade, we have to open up patches of forest. If we leave it alone, the forest will change towards the next seral stage dominated by tolerant species which may not fulfill management objectives. Any such silvicultural treatment for production as a primary objective must be undertaken in balance with non-alteration uses i.e. a balance between production and preservation.

We must be concerned with the manner in which we go about applying this seemingly drastic silvicultural option. The following example should help clarify the matter. Consider a forest area to be managed as a sustainable unit, with a total area of 50,000 acres. Let's assume a rotation (time from establishing a new "crop" until harvesting) of 100 years. Also we'll assume that not all of the forest unit is to be put under productive management due to requirements to preserve biodiversity, inadequate soils or slopes (erosion potential). Hence 30,000 acres would be managed using a clearcutting scheme. Every year 300 acres would be harvested in, for example, ten 30-acre patches which would then be "regenerated" (reforested) either by natural seeding or more likely by planting young seedlings. At the end of the first year, 300 acres of the total 50,000 acres (0.6 %) would have been clearcut. By the end of the tenth year 3,000 acres (6 % of the total management unit) will have been clearcut and regenerated. The oldest plantation (planted patch) would then be around nine years old, assuming that a year is needed for site preparation and planting. This is an over-simplified example of forest regulation. The math is really simple. I think that the logic is as well.

What we've done in our example is to impose restrictions on our clear cutting to make it compatible with other uses. The un-touched 20,000 acres could be destined to protect springs and streams or to afford cover for wildlife. We won't get to the last ten clear cut patches until the 100th year. By that time the first ten patches will have had a 100 years to recover and grow. During the first some 10 or 20 years after clearcutting the opened area will also probably have more food for wildlife (such as grass and shrubs) for browsing than may have been available in the original forest stand. To achieve credibility, multi-participatory (meaning different parties, including "watch-dog" organizations, not directly involved in management) monitoring should be undertaken.

The bottom line: Forest management planning must be based on clearly defined objectives and sound ecological principles using silvicultural options that range from selection systems to clear cutting systems. Restrictions can be imposed on one use, timber in this case, to assure that other uses won't be negatively affected. Sustainability must be in terms of ecological (environmental), economic and social considerations. Clearcutting is a valid option in sustainable forest management when we are dealing with shade-intolerant species.

Jumping from clearcutting to preservation may seem like a disconnect. However as we have just seen, completely removing forest stands in patches can be a means of preserving shade intolerant tree species. Also change happens in forests that are left alone. Preserving does not mean keeping the same forest conditions over time. So, is preservation really sustainable?

Is preservation sustainable?

Preservation is sustainable if you accept change. *The Taos News – Natural Resources Notebook. Jan 10 – 16, 2008*

Can we protect, for example, an area of forest without any sort of human alteration and expect it to remain pretty much the same over relatively long periods of time?

Whether we like it or not, nature's way is to constantly change things, either gradually or often quite abruptly. As an example, we might truly appreciate a beautiful dense old-growth forest and we would like that forest to remain pristine "forever". We might think that if we exclude human extractive activity (such as timber harvesting) we can preserve it in its present condition. What we probably will not perceive is that the forest is gradually changing. The processes of change are natural, mainly through tree growth and the natural death of branches and whole trees that accumulate on the ground. If the main tree species that make up the canopy are shade tolerant then our forest probably is

---

in an advanced, maybe the climax seral stage of ecological succession in which new trees are constantly "being born" to replace those that die of old age (you are invited to go back and look at our previous articles on clearcutting and discussion of Ecological succession defined as "The gradual and orderly process of change in an ecosystem brought about by the progressive replacement of one community by another until a stable climax is established" from: http://www.thefreedictionary.com/ecological+succession).

In our Carson National Forest the most typical forest assemblage is spruce-fir, mostly on north-facing slopes (aspect)at lower elevations and on any exposure at higher elevations. It is generally considered a climax stage in which the forest's over-all composition remains pretty much the same over time until a major catastrophe such as fire takes place. So, as we strive to preserve our forest, little by little it is creating conditions for its own demise. It is not a question of if but of when a fire will occur, either by natural or human causes. Either way, the slow processes and abrupt changes are natural events since it is the combination of growth and death (fuel build up), climatic and weather conditions that can lead to an intense fire, which will create conditions favorable for other tree species, the intolerants, to take over. A new, completely different, forest will be established. We will not have been successful in preserving what we perceived to have been the "original" forest. Even with the best fire control techniques, we will not be able to keep this from happening.

Now let's consider a different type of forest that we might want to preserve. This time we have a forest made up of intolerant species such as aspen. Our example is a beautiful forest of almost pure aspen. Here also change is taking place but now on two fronts. The first is growth as in the previous case. The second, if we look carefully, is a change in the composition of the forest. The young replacement trees (regeneration individuals) are not aspen since that species cannot grow in shade. We will most likely find that the replacement trees are spruce and fir, which are shade tolerant and can effectively compete for space under the aspen canopy. If we extend our imagination a few decades into the future we can see that the forest will change from our beautiful aspen that we wanted to preserve to an equally beautiful spruce-fir forest. Again this takes place through ecological succession and renders useless our efforts to preserve the aspen forest. If we really want to preserve the aspen forest, we must intervene in order to create conditions favorable to that species. This means some form of intensive tree harvesting to keep the stand open so that an intolerant species like aspen can sustain itself. In this case, clearcutting would be an effective means of preservation!

"Preservation" of a forest can be sustainable if we are willing to accept change and if we take into consideration not just one type of forest assemblage covering a relatively small area, but an area large enough to accommodate various species and forest types. Preservation in this sense can also accommodate human extractive techniques, such as logging, in the framework of sustainable forest management which imposes restrictions that promote forest health and well-being for other uses such as water production (watershed management), wildlife (an important part of biodiversity) and recreation which allows people to enjoy our ever-changing forests.

Again, special thanks to Debbie Ragland, UNM-Taos Geology, for her valuable contribution in reviewing and editing.

Aspen (*Populus tremuloides*) is an example of a shade intolerant species. Delving into its ecology will clarify the previous statements regarding its preservation. How do you preserve something that is part of a continuous process of natural transformation?

Aspen: Is nature going to clear-cut it?

The Taos News – Natural Resources Notebook. Oct 9 – 15, 2008. p. C5

Watch for changes in our aspen forests.

As we have discussed in previous articles, nature doesn't like things to remain the same. Our forest ecosystems are no exception. They are constantly changing, in most cases very gradually, in others quite drastically in much more notable situations. Nature has its way of "clearcutting", usually by fire, but also through disease and insects, which paves the way for new vegetation to get established in a "healing" process that is called ecological succession.

In the near future, some or most of our beautiful quaking aspen (Populus tremuloides Michx.) old-growth stands may be in the process, of being "clearcut" by a combination of disease and insects referred to as SAD: sudden aspen decline caused by a "cocktail" of five elements referred to as a "perfect storm" in the Taos News issue of Sept 11-17 by Jim Worrall. So, unfortunately for us, but fortunately for other plant communities that are waiting to "take over" the aspen stands, we may expect to see some harsh changes in our mountain landscapes. This has already happened in Colorado and is notable around the La Veta area. The advance of the disease and insect infestation may have been temporarily hindered by our Sangre de Cristo Mountains, but there is little doubt that it will get to our area. On a recent drive up to Valle Vidal, what I saw, beyond the beauty of the forest and meadows, was the extent of the apparent infestation of aspen. Literally all the trunks are affected up to four or five feet height from the ground. Is this the beginning of the SAD "perfect storm"? The recent Taos News article is a warning to us and preparation so that we won't be surprised by the "invasion" and drastic effects it will have on our mountain landscapes and so that we will hopefully be willing to allow actions to be taken where possible.

We'll take a slight digression from our discussion of aspen to mention another case, this time nature's "clearcutting" of lodgepole pine (Pinus contorta L.) stands by a combination of mountain pine beetle and fire mostly on the western slopes in Colorado. The beetle infestation is spreading to the eastern slopes of the mountains, where lodgepole forest stands are visibly affected at present. The combination is a result of pine beetle mortality which creates fuel conditions for major fires. However, this is not the end of the story. The "clearcut" areas are renewed through ecological succession in a special way in which new lodgepole stands are established. Lodgepole pine needs fire to reproduce. The cones are referred to as serotinous, meaning the need for an external agent such as fire for them to release their seeds. Fire is part of its ecology, so to speak. So nature has its own renewal mechanisms built-in in the case of lodgepole.

These natural phenomena of change should lead us to re-consider how we manage our forests, whether the objective is for preservation or production. We need both in some sort of optimal balance. Too much preservation, not allowing forest management practices, will mean that forest products and economic activity are sacrificed, only to have nature bring about major alterations in which these valuable resources are lost and at the same time result in releasing large quantities of carbon dioxide (the burning of woody plant matter releases CO_2, ash and moisture) thus contributing to the greenhouse effect and global climate change.

If we clearcut before nature does, at least where it is economically viable (do-able), maybe we can save some of our aspen. If nature is going to "clearcut" our old-growth aspen, we would do well to do it first on selected stands and areas. Think of it, the silvicultural practice of clearcutting as a means of preservation!

Whatever we decide to do, forest health is the primary consideration. Our many benefits from our forest ecosystems, ranging from water, aesthetic and atmospheric values to wildlife and wood products, depend on keeping our forests healthy to the greatest extent possible. All forms of management endeavors, from preservation to extractive management, have costs as well as benefits. A healthy balance between what we want to do and what we can do economically is the best strategy.

Natural recuperation from apparently catastrophic events such as fire is a characteristic, a very positive attribute of forest ecosystems. Bouncing back is something that is often overlooked when we observe natural or human-made phenomena. Forest ecosystem resilience is a powerful thing. It's very much a part of forest power.

Forest ecosystem resilience:
Forest Power

FOREST ECOSYSTEM RESILIENCE

Forests: Resilient living entities that grow, recuperate

The Taos News – Natural Resources Notebook. Sep 11 - 17, 2008. p. B11

We may not notice but our forests are growing all the time. Whether we think that it's good or not, our forests constantly proceed to get thicker as a result of the sum of individual trees being born and growing. The question is: What do we want to do with growth?

Continuous growth is offset by tree mortality and damage from natural causes such as old age. Just like any living thing, trees get old, pass on, fall over and give way to news ones. Alterations of different sizes stimulate new growth. Such alterations include small openings created when an individual tree falls or is blown over, taking others with it. This is the most common event. It takes place all the time giving the forest an additional (besides birth and growth) set of dynamics, which serve to keep the forest diverse. This is because tree and other plant species have different degrees of shade tolerance and other habitat preferences. The less shade-tolerant species of grasses, herbs, shrubs and trees take advantage of these openings to get established and grow. They are "healers". Diversity is in terms of age and size structure as well as species and genetic diversity. However, even with this process of gap dynamics, forest stands tend to grow until they reach the habitat's carrying capacity. Once there, theoretically net growth (the difference between over-all growth and mortality) stops. In order for any major growth to take place nature and humans create larger alterations, usually in the form of fire, insects, disease, or any combination of them. The question is, could we or should we remove woody tissue for our benefit while at the same time stimulating growth? We could get wood for energy, for building, furniture or art before nature gets it either by decomposition or fire.

What to "do" can mean different things, but in a nutshell there are two options: the first is not to do anything which may appear attractive; the second is to do something with our forests' net growth. If we harvest growth, even on only a small portion of our public and private forests for energy in the form of biofuel (beyond firewood) in a sustainable manner, it would be a part of our over-all energy policy of gradually substituting foreign oil in our quest for energy independence and for the environment.

Productive sustainability means that we harvest no more than the forest's net growth. This sounds simple but in the real world it is quite complicated. Environmental sustainability essentially means that whatever we do to the forest it must not be detrimental to the total forest habitat or environment, essentially biological diversity and soil. Climate would be another element which is relevant on a large scale. The third aspect of sustainability is that regarding human populations. This is social sustainability which includes political and cultural aspects of human endeavor and means that benefits to human society should outweigh the costs and that, for the most part, people are satisfied.

We must take into account that whatever we want the forest for, it is constantly growing. If we wish to preserve the forest without any physical extraction i.e. wood products, we should consider how we are going to handle forest growth. Once carrying capacity has been reached, growth only takes place to replace biomass lost to mortality. Trees that die of old age or through competition in the forest stand become deadfall. Trunks branches and leaves are subject to decay. However, in dry climates decay is a slow process that tends not to keep up with mortality. The result is a gradual build up of dead wood until something happens to alter the equation. In nature that "something" is usually fire.

Harvesting the net growth of a forest, before it reaches carrying capacity, without causing damage to the ecosystem would provide human society with benefits which it wants and supports while maintaining a healthy forest. We can accept this if we realize that forests are resilient living entities that grow and recuperate from alterations. They produce goods and services that can be obtained permanently, in a sustainable manner, if we harvest in such a way as to not exceed growth and also so as not to damage or deteriorate their habitat.

Again, there is no easy answer. There are trade-offs in anything we do, even doing nothing.

Special thanks to Debbie Ragland, UNM-Taos Geology, for her valuable contribution in reviewing and editing.

How resiliency works in forest ecosystems

The Taos News – Natural Resources Notebook. Oct 7 - 13, 2010. p. B9

Watching forest ecosystems' responses to events such as fire is fascinating, if you have enough time. In our area at lower elevations, it's a slow process. At higher elevations you can actually see things happening. Systematic multi-party monitoring is a process that requires organization, resources and the will to stay with it. Through it we can see how forest ecosystems have responded to past events.

Resiliency can be thought of as a healing process. How does it work? What makes it happen? The answers can be summed up in two key words (and concepts): biodiversity and soil. Forest ecosystems need to have a source of replenishment of a variety of "healers", plant species that are in charge of establishing a cover and starting the slow process of ecological succession. They obviously need a habitat in which the healers can flourish. Soil is the key factor in that habitat. If the soil is relatively unaltered and the seed and sprout sources are available, the conditions are right for the ecosystem to show its resiliency. Healers come in all forms, from very small plants to grasses, shrubs and trees.

Biological diversity means that there is a range of different species of plants and animals that play different roles in the dynamic processes of living things in communities, which are complex associations. Ecologists refer to the roles as ecological niches. Like a complex machine, the different pieces fit together, interacting to have a given way of behaving: system behavior. An important part of system behavior is how a system or ecosystem responds to external stimuli. A specific stimulus can be gradual, such as climate change, or sudden as in the case of fire.

What is stimulus? We think of economics, recession and programs for recovery. In ecology, stimulus is a factor, a thing that happens, that provokes a reaction. In the systems approach, we consider something from outside the system, a stimulus, which causes it to react in some way. Systems ecology is the science that uses this approach to study and understand ecosystems.

A stimulus can also be in the form of forest treatment in the context of sustainable productive forest management, which should be in balance with non-extractive forest management. Silvicutural treatment is based on sound ecological principles that must take into account all components of the ecosystem: plant and animal, large, small and microscopic. Resiliency is a major factor. Sustainable means that responses are adequate to maintain productivity (soil, stocking level and biodiversity).

Retroactive monitoring is not simple but it's needed for evaluation and for public credibility in sustainable productive forest management. It involves looking for situations where events took place some time ago and seeing how the ecosystems have responded.

Habitat plays an important role in resilience. In general in a better habitat the healing process takes place faster. On the Hondo Burn, over 9,000 feet we can see it greening, mostly with Gambel Oak and Aspen. But at lower elevation near San Cristobal, what we see is mostly grass, except on the north-facing slopes of the small canyons where the oak is quite dense. The harsher the habitat, the slower the healing process is. Under harsher conditions more caution must be used, meaning disturbances must be kept at a lower level. Resilience is there but at a slow pace.

A great source: www.cbd.int/doc/publications/cbd-ts-43-en.pdf

Some provocative terms: ecological resilience and engineering resilience.

Forest ecosystem resilience can be observed and monitored. This can be done directly by setting up a network of observation points, preferably permanent plots that can be measured periodically over long periods of time. An indirect approach involves selecting areas that have been altered in the past through timber harvesting or fire and re-creating their history from records on the ground and from remote sensing (aerial photography and satellite imaging). This could be referred to as retroactive monitoring.

Demo areas in forest treatment monitoring

The Taos News – Natural Resources Notebook. Sep 23 - 29, 2010. p. B5

Have past forest harvesting (logging) practices been good or bad? Demonstration areas can show how forest ecosystems are resilient.

Forest ecosystems are living entities and as such react to what happens to them and to their habitat. Response to alterations of different intensities is part of their inherent capabilities that have evolved over long periods of time as a means of survival. That's what resiliency means. In general it can be said that species such as our ponderosa pine, blue spruce or aspen have found ways to survive a wide range of catastrophes. Probably the most common is fire. Going further in our thinking, individual genetic makeup wants to survive in individuals and in their associations in communities of living things, in ecosystems. Our genes and those of trees want to perpetuate themselves through survival and reproduction.

So what happens when an apparently destructive event like fire happens to a forest: Is it lost forever? The answer is no, or else there wouldn't be any forests. Forests regenerate themselves through a wide variety of mechanisms. The bottom line is ecosystem resiliency, closely associated with soil health and biodiversity.

A picture is worth a hundred words and a real-life setting is worth a hundred pictures. Multi-party monitoring, or for that matter any monitoring, requires training, which can be in the form of written and verbal communication supported by real situations where one can see, feel, hear, smell the forest setting. In living and appreciating such an experience, knowledge of the history of that particular forest stand is a must. Wouldn't it be good if we had a set of forest demonstration areas ranging from undisturbed forests to the most altered situations imaginable (intense fire, clearcutting)? Maybe we do have this but if so, it's not well known to the general public.

Undisturbed areas should be easy to find in our Carson National Forest and privately owned forests in the area. Finding documented altered areas is a more difficult matter. We know about areas where timber harvesting took place years ago. It would be good to be able to see these areas 50 years later. We could see how each forest ecosystem has responded to, for instance, possible over-cutting. This would include observing soil conditions as well as forest stands. We would be looking for regeneration (new born trees) and health and growth of surviving trees, some of which may have been scarred during harvesting.

To get the most out of this we would need to know what the stand was like before treatment (logging) took place. We would also need to know how much timber was removed and how much of the remaining stand was damaged by the logging process. Finally it would be great to know what the remaining stand was like. Describing what it was like involves qualitative information regarding number of trees per acre, their distribution by size (diameter classes) and the basal area of the stand. Basal area is the sum of the cross-sections taken at 4.5 feet height on the trunk, calculated from measuring diameter (DBH).

In an ITTO project in Venezuelan tropical forests, we proposed what we called the "pre-post" forest monitoring model using a combination of one-time (static) inventories (temporary plot samples) and dynamic sampling using permanent plots that can be measured periodically.

Retroactive monitoring is not simple but it's needed for evaluation and for public credibility in sustainable productive forest management.

Forest ecosystem resilience and sustainability go together

Effective, transparent, objective multiparty monitoring of forest ecosystems' response to events is essential for sustainability and for credibility. For sustainability, it's how forest management interdisciplinary teams evaluate and correct treatment. For credibility it's how the public, through third party watch-dog, groups can gain confidence in forest management. Even for sustainable non-extractive forest management (SNEFM), sustainability is not guaranteed and monitoring is necessary to know how protected ecosystems are changing.

SUSTAINABILITY

Sustainability in forest management is a wide (and controversial) subject. The idea here is to share some ideas on it without pretending for it to be an essay on sustainability. One of the ideas is regarding how forest managers can achieve sustainability through measures that regulate practices. Imposing restrictions is part of the planning process. Following up on specific practices that have taken place in the past is another element. At the planning stage projections are made as to how the forest ecosystems will respond to treatment. In the follow-up monitoring process the real response must be compared to the projections in order to make adjustments and to serve as a basis for future decision-making and public knowledge and, especially, credibility. To enhance credibility, monitoring must involve a wide range of actors: multi-party monitoring.

Imposing restrictions to achieve sustainability in forest management

Restrictions on achieving sustainability in forest management. *The Taos News – Natural Resources Notebook. June 5 – 11, 2008. p. B11.*

In our discussion on thinning a forest that is too thick, especially if we need to remove large trees as well as smaller ones, one might ask: What will happen to wildlife, such as the spotted owl, deer or wild turkeys? What will happen or what we think will happen is a major concern in achieving sustainability in all its ramifications. Our first objective should be to understand the ecology / biology of any species about which we are concerned. For instance, knowing the spotted owl population in our forest and its needs for survival is a pre-requisite in planning our thinning. We should answer such questions as: What kind of tree does the spotted owl need for nesting and how many trees should there be per acre? What should the forest floor be like to support sufficient food? The same is true for any target species, be it plant or animal. Once we have this information, we can formulate a set of conditions that will act as restrictions on tree removal. Modeling territorial restrictions is not an easy task, but the data is, in most cases, available or can be gathered by multidisciplinary efforts. Of course, the easy way out would be to eliminate tree cutting, in effect, using the spotted owl as a pretext to stop thinning that involves large trees. But "easy solutions" may not result in the desired outcomes; stopping large tree removal does not guarantee sustainability. As we have said before, there are no easy answers in forest ecology and management.

Now, let's consider an entire hypothetical forest system. We will assume that we own the forest and that we can do anything we want with it. First, we must state that it is our policy that the forest is to remain forever; that anything we do must be sustainable. Let us assume that our primary goal is to operate a small timber industry, but the forest is also to be multi-purpose. We resolve that wildlife, recreational opportunities, and aesthetic values will be sustained in our forest, therefore timber production must not negatively impact these entities, activities, or values. We can further complicate the scenario by assuming that our forest is a watershed for one of our acequia systems. It now becomes imperative that we protect the watershed by further restricting tree harvesting.

Now let's really throw a monkey wrench into the works. Let's assume that we have commercially accessible natural gas and/or oil beneath our forest. Can we drill and produce energy resources and at the same time achieve sustainability in the terms that we have established? The answer in part depends on the economics of natural gas or oil production under the severe drilling, pumping and transport (electric and pipe line) restrictions needed to ensure that hydrocarbon production is not detrimental to our water, timber and wildlife. With gas and diesel at around four dollars a gallon and crude oil over a $100 a barrel, what is our decision? Is it worth the effort to sustain our forest under the conditions we have established?

Finally, let's assume that our forest actually belongs to a large group of people, perhaps a community or a medium-sized business. Our job as forest managers along with the water suppliers, wildlife administrators, and the petroleum industry is to maintain a credible enterprise. We will have "watch-dog" groups who have vested interests in ecology, business, wildlife management, and recreation who will monitor our endeavors to make sure that we are achieving our goals of environmental, economic and socio-political sustainability. It is now clear that achieving forest sustainability involves willingness to accept many complications and avoiding simplistic "easy-way-out" solutions.

Balance is an essential element of sustainability. Anything out on the fringes is most likely unsustainable in forest management, our daily lives and in politics.

Sustainable productive forest management (SPFM) and sustainable non-extractive forest management (SNEFM) are two complementary approaches to dealing with our forest ecosystems. In balance, they are a major factor in over-all environmental, economic and socio-political sustainability.

**Balance is key to
sustainability**

Striking a balance in forest management

The Taos News – Natural Resources Notebook. July 31– Aug. 6, 2008. p. B15

Is it possible for forest preservation and productive management to co-exist?

Striking a balance between opposing matters is the key to better living, both in our daily lives and in more transcendental matters such as natural resource allocation and management. Trade-off situations are common in forest management just like in our everyday life. An example of such trade-off situations is whether to use our forest resources or preserve them: sustainable productive forest management (mainly but not exclusively for wood products) vs. sustainable preservation management. We should not consider it an "either or" dilemma but rather a combination with compromise; in short, striking a favorable balance that provides the most satisfaction to the most people in our complex modern society. Thus the idea of an optimum balance as a strategy of solving our "use it" vs. "preserve it" conflicts. One aspect of the problem is a change of attitude on the part of both sides towards finding common ground which should be possible since the overall objective is the same: that forest ecosystems remain forever for the benefit of human society. Another aspect of the strategy lies in land use planning that takes into account the characteristics and potential of forest resources on one hand while on the other hand taking into account the needs, desires and preferences of human society.

Such a balance can be and is achieved through land use planning on national, regional, state, local levels meaning designation of broad areas for different uses and/or combinations of uses and through measures taken within specific forest units, whether public or private. This constitutes achieving a balance on a broad scale and on a local scale within public or private forest holdings. We have, or at least had, large areas designated for production in combination with other uses (our national forests) and areas designated for preservation in the form of wilderness areas, national parks, wildlife refuges, etc. However, recently the trend has been to tip the balance more toward preservation at the expense of production. This may be what modern society has wanted but the final outcome may well prove to be quite different than expected. In any case the objective is sustainability.

The underlying principle is forest ecology. Both preservation and productive management are based on knowledge, still far from complete, of the complex relationships among elements of forest ecosystems. We might be inclined to think that we should wait until we have full knowledge before we decide to use forest resources. However, not using them does not guarantee that they will in effect be preserved. By the same token over-using would not be a good idea either. The precautionary principle applies in that productive use must allow for wide safety margins. The bottom line: striking a balance. Our modern society has needs, some of which can be satisfied through productive management based on sound ecological principles. Wood is a renewable option for a wide variety of uses including energy. Imagine if we could harvest even a small portion of our forests' overall growth as part of our alternative energy strategy. The potential is great not only for energy but also for sustainable economic development in terms of jobs that can't be outsourced.

Planning makes use of information on habitat, existing forest types (ecosystems), land and other resource use patterns or trends by the population, and projections of future needs. Once land use potentials are determined, land resources can be assigned for different types of use. A balance can then be arrived at by combining use and preservation within a given use potential area. In other words, a given forest area designated for production can be divided between actual use under sustainable principles and forest areas set aside under preservation management of areas in which no forest goods are extracted. For example, a given national forest, such as the Carson, could be zoned so as to designate a large part of the area for preservation management with a smaller portion designated for multiple objective production. Then, within the areas designated for production, certain areas could be left untouched to preserve forest types that might not be represented in the preserved area. Forest areas designated for production would be managed under certain restrictions to make it compatible with other uses such as water.

All this sounds complicated, but who would venture to say that forest management is simple or can be made simple? Again, there are no simple answers. Trying to preserve too much (out of balance) will not work in the long run.

**Balance, sustainability
and more balance**

Balance is key to healthy forests

The Taos News – Natural Resources Notebook. Sep 9 – 15, 2010. p. B5

Balance is an important thing in life, in almost all our matters, ranging from politics to diet. In politics, neither too liberal nor too conservative is sustainable in governing a society. It may work for a while but being out of balance will end up self-destructing. The same is true regarding our forest resources. A large part of over-all sustainability has to do with balance. For something to be sustainable, it usually must not be out in the fringes: not out of balance.

Here we re-visit: "Striking a Balance in Forest Management", The Taos News Natural Resources Notebook of July 31, 2008.

If we over-use our forest resources, then it obviously will not be sustainable. Surprisingly, the same is true regarding over-protecting. Trying to protect too much is not sustainable. It may work for a while but society in general needs tangible benefits, meaning jobs and economic growth. Furthermore, in over-protecting, not allowing extractive use of our public forests, we're losing vast amounts of resources to insect, disease and fire. Yellowstone Park forests are turning brown from the mountain pine (bark) beetle (*Dendroctonus ponderosae*) infestation in whitebark pine (*Pinus albicalus*) See "Beetle Devastates Yellowstone Whitebark Pine Forests" (http://www.actionbioscience.org/environment/loganmacfarlane.html).

Another example: In Colorado west of Fort Collins extensive areas of

lodgepole pine forests are suffering what has been referred to as a "...
perfect storm resulting in the intensive mountain pine beetle outbreak
..." as stated in "Mountain Pine Beetles in Colorado" (http://www.fs.fed.
us/rmrs/bark-beetle/faq/). The authors cite three factors: extensive
uninterrupted forest stands, drought and mild winters. Climate change
is considered an issue. Overstocking (forest that are too thick) probably
is a factor.

The next step will be fire in the stands of dead dry trees. This can be
considered nature's way of renewing them, but obviously preservation is
not working. We can say: "OK, we'll leave it to Nature". The dynamics of
lot of natural forest ecosystem processes, such as "catastrophic" changes
by fire, are not pretty. What I think most people want to preserve are
the attractive forest ecosystems, our mixed conifer and aspen forests, as
they are.

Letting Nature take its course on too much of our public forests is out of
balance, just as it would be to try to alter too much of our forests. The
sustainable option is a balance between non-extractive forest management
and sustainable productive management, where "productive" means some
form of extraction. When we think of forest management, what first comes
to mind is logging and wood products industries. However, setting aside
areas of forest, such as our wilderness areas, is also forest management.
Forest management is based on sound ecological knowledge. We must
know and understand forest ecosystem dynamics if we are going to manage
them, even if such management is for preservation. Forest ecosystems are
constantly changing, mostly at a slow pace that we can't see. Trees grow,
die and are born constantly. Forest ecosystems are living entities, like our
bodies, made up of many living things: our cells and the microorganisms
that live inside us. They reproduce, grow, live and die constantly and we
remain healthy (until something gets out of balance). Likewise, forests
don't cease to exist because some trees die or are removed. Even groups
of trees can be removed by nature or by humans and the forest will heal.
The key: resilience.

CLIMATE CHANGE AND FOREST ECOLOGY AND MANAGEMENT

The effect that forest management can have on climate change mitigation has to do with the Carbon cycle. Carbon in CO_2 is taken up by forests through photosynthesis and converted to carbohydrates (C-H-O; basically sugars) part of which in turn are converted into plant tissue – wood- and stored as such. Another part is consumed in respiration releasing CO_2 and providing energy for plant cells. Trees emit more O_2 than CO_2.

But first, let's think about the complex matter of arriving at good measures of temperature as a basis for considering global climate change.

Taking the Earth's temperature

Taking the earth's temperature a complicated process. *The Taos News – Natural Resources Notebook. Feb 28 – Mar 5, 2008. p. C10*

The general consensus among scientists and much of the general public is that our biosphere is warming. Global warming is real. However, the consensus ends when we try to determine how much it is warming and even more so, why it is.

Firstly, "global" refers to all of something. What something? In this case, it is not the earth as a whole. The core and mantle probably are not warming – at least we better hope not! Of course we are referring to the part that we and other living things live in: the biosphere, which encompasses the lower atmosphere, the oceans and the earth's surface, i.e. where life exists. What is the Earth's temperature (in terms of definition and degrees)? Warming means that temperature is increasing, so the problem to address is how to take the temperature of something so large and complex as our biosphere to determine its rate of change.

How can we arrive at an "average" temperature at a given time and then compare it over time to determine how fast it is changing? These questions are the root of much speculation and, needless to say, much disagreement. So we have two elements of a major complex problem. The

---

first, arriving at a global average temperature which means having a series of "reporting stations" at which we measure and record temperature. The second element is determining how this average temperature changes over time. Unfortunately, the Earth has no tongue under which we can put a thermometer!

When we can't measure the whole of something, we take a set of samples that is supposed to be representative. However, three-quarters of the Earth's surface and hence the biosphere's volume is made up of the oceans. Another similar problem is difficultly in accessing remote mountain ranges, deserts, the Artic, the Antarctic and other generally inhospitable areas. How do we measure temperatures in these remote or nearly inaccessible places? An additional problem: how do we distribute the data points? Do we use the currently existing reporting stations distributed unevenly throughout the world or do we attempt to set up evenly-distributed stations on land and sea? This comprises a sampling problem which can lead to vastly different statistical results. Our sample set is made up of sample units (our data points) which are the individual places at which data (in this case, temperature) is recorded. (Sampling is an important tool in natural resources management. It allows us to estimate an attribute of a given resource such as the volume of timber in a forest or the deer population in a given area.) In setting up our sampling locations we are supposed to avoid bias, which means that we are not to have any pre-determined preference as to where the individual sample units are located. To avoid a biased outcome, we should use either a random or a systematic scheme of selection. If we choose places that are easy to measure or that we feel "best represent" each local condition, then we have a biased sample that will not reflect the real situation. Unfortunately, most of our climate reporting stations are located with a great deal of bias. These stations are often located at airports which are almost always near cities or towns. As a result, any average temperature that we calculate from these samples is biased and will not truly reflect the average temperature of our Earth's biosphere.

The second problem is how to average over time. One very hot summer or very cold winter (like now) does not mean we are warming or cooling. Do we average over five-year intervals? Do we average over historic intervals (hundreds to thousands of years)? Do we average over geologic intervals (millions of years)? What time interval will best reflect the trend in climate change? Complications and subjectivity can also be introduced at this stage. What we are considering here is the problem of spatial and temporal (time) temperature variations. Variation is the complicating element in trying to characterize something. For example, if all trees in a forest were the same size and distributed in a uniform pattern (i.e. the number of trees per acre would be the same in all places) sampling would be easy. A single sample unit would be enough. In this case variation would be zero (non-existent). How do we take into account variation? The answer is: Statistics.

Our global sample of temperature data points is biased, probably towards the higher temperatures because most data points are located near urban areas that are almost certainly warmer than rural areas. There is no one easy or correct objective way to take our biosphere's temperature, which leads to controversy and confusion. On the other hand, we have indirect indications of warming such as rate of glacier retreat and coral formations. These are just a very few reasons as to why there is so much disagreement on global warming – and we didn't even get to the "why" part!

Again, special thanks to Debbie Ragland, UNM-Taos Geology, for her valuable contribution in reviewing and editing.

Global warming and forest management

Global warming and forest health. *The Taos News – Natural Resources Notebook. Oct 18 – 24, 2007. pp. B10, B11*

This was the first article in the Natural Resources Notebook series.

Have you ever thought about how the way in which we manage forests could be related to global warming?

Natural Resource Management is a fascinating field which involves science and its application in dealing with problems that range from how to manage forests, natural parks, rangelands and watersheds to elements of global climate change, more popularly known as global warming. As such we can refer to a relatively new field: "environmental management", which involves applying knowledge obtained from environmental science to specific manageable aspects in order to produce results that improve our environment. For instance, one possible area would be related to how forest management practices can be implemented to mitigate greenhouse gas emissions that contribute to global warming. We can think of how trees and other plants in the forest absorb carbon dioxide (CO_2) through photosynthesis, which is the process by which CO_2 is converted to "food" for plants using solar energy, water and nutrients from the soil. If we can determine how much Carbon is "fixed" into plant tissues such as the cellulose in wood, then we can develop policies through which CO_2 emissions can be offset to a degree by managing forests and other vegetation. This involves the idea of carbon taxes and carbon credits in environmental management which combines science with technology, economics and even politics (hello Al Gore). Carbon as a chemical element is the culprit, but it is also one of the main elements that we and all known living things are made of and a lot of what we eat.

Science describes the carbon cycle in which the element goes from its form of CO_2 gas to food, carbohydrates that are made by most plants and is also food for those same plants as well as food and fiber for animals. Through respiration (our breathing) oxygen is used by most living organisms, both plant and animal and CO_2 is emitted. By the way, our simple act of breathing contributes to global warming!

Forests play a significant role in absorbing CO_2 which is related to growth. The more growth the more Carbon is "fixed" in woody tissues in trees and shrubs. In general it can be assumed that a young forest, for example one that is in the process of re-establishing itself after a fire, will grow more rapidly than and older forest. In this sense in a more mature forest we are referring to growth as a means of replacing tree trunks, branches and roots that are lost or damaged in natural aging process of individual trees and in the forest community as a whole. We can use the term net growth which is the difference between the rate of such woody tissue replacement growth and the rate of tissue loss, i.e. trees that die, branches that are broken, etc. In an older mature forest net growth may be near zero since the forest is near the carrying capacity of its environment i.e. soil, climate. In a young forest that is occupying new space opened up by a fire new growth exceeds tissue loss (during the growing process after the disturbance). Consequently CO_2 absorption is greater. However, the downside is that the fire released CO_2 from the Carbon that was stored in woody tissues! Now, if instead of fire, the woody tissue were to be removed for non-combustion uses such as lumber, poles, cardboard etc. through forest management practices, instead of a fire, we would have a net gain in CO_2 fixation (absorption) thus contributing to greenhouse gas emission reduction.

 FOREST POWER Adventures in Ecology and Forest Management

Global dimming: An inconvenient complication?

Co-author: Debbie Ragland. The Taos News – Natural Resources Notebook. Jan 24 - 30, 2008

Could global "dimming" to some degree offset global warming from greenhouse gas emissions or does it compound the problem of global climate change?

We have all heard a lot about global warming due to the greenhouse effect caused by the increase in carbon dioxide, methane and other gasses that we (and nature) are putting into our atmosphere, but what do we hear about global cooling that may also be caused in part by atmospheric pollution? In a nutshell, global "dimming" is a cooling effect caused by particle pollution (mostly industrial emissions but also, for example, jet plane contrails and volcanoes) that increases our atmosphere's solar energy reflectivity.

A complex exchange of radiation is at work in our Earth-Sun system: the sun beams ultraviolet (short-wave) and visible radiation to the Earth and the Earth radiates long-wave or infrared radiation back towards space. Our atmosphere, with all of its natural (e.g., clouds) and human-introduced (e.g., excessive carbon dioxide) components, intercepts some of this radiation either absorbing or reflecting variable percentages. Excessive radiation back to Earth as clouds and pollution increase contributes to global warming. (The reader is encouraged to consult the many interesting meteorology texts and internet sites for a more comprehensive discussion of the Sun-Earth system radiation budget.)

Part of the sun's energy that is intercepted by our planet is reflected back into space. Scientists refer to an object's albedo as a measure of this reflectivity. In the simplest terms, objects reflect and absorb light (energy) in relation to their color. Light-colored objects such as clouds reflect more energy and thus appear brighter than dark colored objects which absorb more energy and thus appear darker. The planet Venus is bright due to its high degree of reflectivity (its high albedo). In our Earth-Sun system, as increased clouds and/or particulate matter reflect solar input back into space, less solar energy is able to reach the Earth's surface. High reflectance into space means less solar energy available for consumption by life on the surface, and, coincidentally, less solar energy input available for global warming. From the perspective of life on the Earth's surface and the lower atmosphere, this is global "dimming." Paradoxically, what we would see as global dimming on the Earth's surface would be seen as a "brighter" planet (increased albedo) from space.

Particle pollution in our atmosphere can increase the Earth's albedo; as a consequence, more energy may be reflected back into space, thus reducing the energy that could be trapped in the Earth's atmosphere through the greenhouse effect. As a result we have two processes occurring that work in opposite directions. We could jump to the conclusion that global dimming is a good thing and consequently we could worry less about global warming. However, there is a downside. On one hand, global dimming could "mask" (or tend to hide) the overall increased temperature effects of global warming (i.e without the cooling effect of global dimming, global warming would be even greater and more evident). Global dimming could also generate a greater imbalance in global heat distribution thus affecting weather patterns that determine regional climate change (probably not good). Because of greater industrial development in the northern hemisphere, the imbalance between the northern and southern hemispheres could be significantly increased. And, excessive global dimming could lead to a feedback loop, that is, our planet could significantly cool (in the long run or short run?) rather than warm. This would not be the first time that pollutants in the atmosphere contributed to the cooling of our planet; the demise of the dinosaurs 65 million years ago was caused at least in part by huge amounts of particulate matter thrown into the atmosphere by the asteroid impact. This "dimming" would have led to decreased solar input and a possible temporary cooling of the planet.

The Sun-Earth radiation system and global climate change are very complex subjects. Both human and natural factors interact in ways that we still do not fully understand. We do not know all of the answers; much more research is necessary before we begin to understand all of the intricacies and reactions of our changing world. We do need to take internationally concerted actions to understand and modify our human inputs, which will probably mean sacrifices by everyone, but will, at the same time, create new and exciting opportunities.

Save a tree, use a hand dryer

The Taos News – Natural Resources Notebook. Dec 13 – 19, 2007. p. C10

Does replacing paper towels with air hand dryers in public restrooms really help the environment?

You know, where it says "save a tree". Like most important and relevant things in life the answer is not a simple one. First let's consider where the paper in our paper towels comes from. The electric hand dryer message is based on the assumption that the paper towels come from trees, and ultimately, this is true. Trees are the original source of paper, but some of the paper in towels probably comes from recycled paper products. An import matter to consider is that while trees grow they take carbon dioxide out of the atmosphere, thus mitigating green house gas emissions and global warming. The paper that comes from trees can be further broken down into those grown in natural forest, mostly in Canada for our market source and from trees grown in plantations, largely in our southeast. These forests can be further broken down into those harvested in sustainable forest management vs. trees taken from forest areas that are converted to non-forest uses, i.e. roads, building sites, farm or ranch land. The latter type of harvesting is a sporadic non-sustainable source which may or may not contribute significantly.

We can ask what kind of management practices are implemented in the first case. Bulk, low per-unit value wood is most likely harvested in relatively pure forest stands in which the whole "crop" is harvested at one time. This is known as clearcutting (sometimes written "clear-cutting"). In the framework of sustainable forest management, it takes place in a patch or quilt-like pattern of areas whose size depends on the regeneration habits of the forest species (part of its ecology), topographic and economic considerations. From a bird's-eye view, the overall area of the forest unit is mostly unaltered. Once an area is harvested, i.e. clear-cut, it is regenerated either naturally or by planting. The idea is to have a cycle (rotation) in which overall growth measured in volume or weight per acre is kept at the maximum afforded by the tree species, soil, climate and cultivation (silvicultural) techniques. Maximum overall growth also means maximum CO_2 absorption from the atmosphere. The underlying principle is that the faster the overall net growth of a forest, the more CO_2 taken from the atmosphere through photosynthesis, which is the conversion of atmospheric Carbon into "food" for the trees in the form of various carbohydrates (basically sugars). Maximum net tree trunk (and some other woody tissues) growth can be the goal whether the forest is regenerated naturally or by planting.

Most paper in the US comes from fast-growing pine plantations that take up CO2 as they grow and are a form of renewable cultivation that amounts to minimal cultivation. Soil is prepared –i.e. plowed- maybe once every 20 years instead of every year or twice a year as in most agricultural crop production, and it is mostly organic! Many of the plantations are on soils previously used to grow tobacco and other crops.

Again, you will notice that I have used "probably" and "it may" which means I do not have all the answers. As my colleagues and I have stated before, we are trying to stimulate thinking on important, complex subjects. We know that the solutions to these problems will not be simple.

The bottom line: Perhaps the more paper towels we use, the more CO2 that will be taken out of the atmosphere, thereby mitigating our greenhouse gas emissions and helping to reduce global warming. However there is a downside: The more paper towels we use, the more energy used to make them and also the more chemicals that go into the pulp and paper production process which also has emissions. There is no easy answer! Life is like that. The initial question remains unanswered.

Again, special thanks to Debbie Ragland, UNM-Taos Geology, for her valuable contribution in reviewing and editing.

If we accept the idea that sustainable productive forest management (SPFM) can contribute to global climate change mitigation, then we need to consider some basic elements of forest treatment. Growth is the net production of forest ecosystems. The idea is that if only the amount of wood that is added on in a given period of time is harvested, this is the first step towards sustainability. This is what foresters used to call sustained yield. It is much like "harvesting" the interest on a savings account, while keeping the principal intact. Further sustainability involves maintaining the productive capacity and health of the forests. This is sort of like taking care of the bank and the banking system while "harvesting" the interest. The bank and its environment is analogous to a forest ecosystem and its surroundings, its environment, including the human environment, which involves economic, social and political well-being.

This leads us to some basic principles and ideas on timber and wood harvesting. Logging is simply the operation in which wood is removed from the forest ecosystem and taken to a wood processing site. Loggers only remove what the forest management team has designated and in the way in which the latter have determined in order to "take care of the bank" looking out for over all sustainability by taking care of the forest ecosystem.

Now on to harvesting the interest: the net growth of a forest ecosystem under SPFM.

HARVESTING FOREST GROWTH

Harvesting forest growth: An option?

The Taos News – Natural Resources Notebook. Dec 18-24, 2008. p. B12

Could we create jobs, maybe as part of the new administration's green energy program, mitigate the fossil energy/global warming problem and improve forest health all in one initiative through growth harvesting? A forest in which there is room to grow, meaning not too thick, will be a healthier forest that is more resistant to fire (less fuel), insect damage (such as bark beetle) and disease. Furthermore, more growth means more carbon dioxide is taken from the atmosphere, which in turn can help offset our fossil fuel carbon emissions.

Would we agree that it is possible to harvest forest growth on selected areas of public forest in such a way that we will actually improve forest health provided that we are careful in establishing the criteria for deciding where and how to go about it? "Where" and "how" mean good land use planning and prescribing adequate forestry practices in the framework of sustainable forest management.

We have said in previous articles that since forests grow, and are effective in recovering from alterations, we might as well try to reap their benefits, at least on a portion of our public forests. We also discussed how to go about harvesting growth and have furthermore suggested that we might be able to get part of our energy needs in this manner while at the same time improving forest health. Now we'll consider how we could decide where to harvest, taking into consideration the fact that such sustainable forest management will not be feasible, nor is it desirable on all areas of our forests. Furthermore, we could start on small areas of forest to give the general public the opportunity to monitor and evaluate the endeavor and gradually increase the scale.

When we say on a part of our public forests, this means that we must have some form of land use planning method in place by which we can select the most suitable forest stands. This means establishing criteria on what "suitable" means in terms of habitat and forest conditions of the ecosystems that we plan to treat. To start with, we must be willing to consider timber harvesting as a silvicultural treatment. We will define the term as: "a practice used to achieve a specific result, which implies some form of modification of the forest ecosystem's structure and composition that is based on sound forest ecology principles and that is an integral part of sustainable forest management".

Practices, such as growth harvesting, will depend on forest conditions regarding both the characteristics of the forest stands (i.e. basal area and diameter distribution) and their habitat. We could start with topography which can be readily obtained from remote sensing (use of satellite images). We would then combine this information with accessibility in terms of distances from existing roads in order to optimize road construction. Roads are needed for management as well as transportation of wood. Additional information that would be combined in the land use planning model includes forest stand characteristics, soils and geomorphology, and areas of special uses such as spiritual retreats, habitat reserves for endangered species, etc. We would "combine" our collected data by overlapping various maps using geographical information systems (GIS), that is, "mapematics", the use of mathematical models in conjunction with digital information that corresponds to data points geographically referenced using coordinates so as to provide the "how much" linked to the "where". This information can be used in system modeling as a tool for decision making.

As we can see, planning makes use of powerful tools that, when combined with human expertise and good judgment, both in the office and on the ground, provide a high degree of confidence and probability of success in achieving sustainability while providing direct benefits to society. The inherent natural resilience of forest ecosystems is a sound foundation on which to build well-planned management endeavors.

The choices to be made may be tough, but doing nothing is probably the worst option. Forest health and its related resistance to nature's and man's elements of abrupt change determine that we seriously consider harvesting forest growth where (in places, specific forest areas) we can be sure of success. Existing forest ecology and forest management science and technology is sufficient to determine where and how to go about it. Public participation in planning, implementation and especially in multi-party monitoring the forest ecosystems' responses is essential. Again, there are no easy answers regarding our natural resources.

Again, special thanks to Debbie Ragland, UNM-Taos Geology, for her valuable contribution in reviewing and editing.

Harvesting our forest ecosystems' growth, at least on a part of our forests, opens up a huge renewable energy potential; one in which environmental services are enhanced while obtaining truly green energy and providing sustainable jobs.

Energy from forests in a comprehensive strategy

Energy from forests a sound strategy. *The Taos News – Natural Resources Notebook. Aug 28 – Sep 3, 2008. p. B9*

Should we include our forests in an over-all energy strategy? If we can figure out a way to convert net forest growth to energy it might end up being a significant part of the renewable energy component along with other biofuels, solar and wind.

Before going into the forest management aspects, let's consider decision-making approaches in the form of strategies in the far broader and more complex energy situation. A strategy is a carefully devised plan of action used to solve important, complex problems often when we have insufficient information and where much is at stake. Our present energy dilemma is just that sort of very important, complex problem where we, at present, have no definite solutions. In the case of our energy problems, we require strategies that are broad enough to cover the many facets of the problem. Energy strategy is a multi-faceted problem in which all possible components, in all manner of combinations must be considered. This is, in a way, an experimental approach. Strategies that are comprehensive, covering a wide range of possible solution approaches, must be flexible in order to adapt to new knowledge and often to major changes in the geopolitical environment. Information input is constant and, in many ways, constantly changing in an environment of uncertainty where many factors are beyond the planners' control. Energy policies are influenced by geopolitical situations such as terrorist attacks or political uncertainties such as nationalizations and changing alliances which can result in policy changes, and by natural events such as hurricanes in the Gulf of Mexico that routinely shut down drilling platforms.

In such complex matters as our energy situation, multiple trade-off situations arise regarding contradictory aspects in which a possible solution usually lies in some form of balance among the conflicting elements. In this setting, our public and private forests may be able to play a major role if we are willing to consider the alternatives. Forests are resilient living entities that grow and react in response to events. They produce goods and services that can be obtained permanently, in a sustainable manner, if we harvest in such a way as to not exceed growth and so as not to damage or deteriorate their habitat, mainly soil, and their biological diversity. If we could economically harvest growth on only a small portion of our public and private forests for energy as a form of biofuel (besides firewood which already is important in our area), just think of how that could enter into the overall equation of gradually substituting foreign and eventually domestic oil in our quest for energy independence and for our environment.

Forest growth can be considered analogous to financial interest where the forest stand is the principal and growth is the interest. If a savings account is to be sustainable, we must not withdraw more than the interest. We must realize that whatever we want the forest for, it is constantly growing. Individual trees are being born (natural regeneration), growing and dying. If we wish to preserve the forest without any physical extraction, i.e. wood products, we should consider how we are going to handle forest growth. In nature, net growth proceeds until some form of limit is reached which would be the carrying capacity. Once that limit has been reached theoretically net growth ceases. Growth then takes place to replace biomass lost to mortality. Trees that die of old age or through competition in the forest stand become deadfall. Trunks, branches and leaves are subject to decay. However, in dry climates decay is a slow process that doesn't keep up with mortality. The result is a gradual build-up of dead wood until something happens to alter the equation. In nature that "something" is usually fire.

The state of forest science and management is such that net forest growth can be harvested on a sustainable basis, that is, without causing damage to the productive potential of the ecosystem and at the same time providing human society with benefits which it wants and supports; in short, contributing to making most of the people happy most of the time.

Again, special thanks to Debbie Ragland, UNM-Taos Geology, for her valuable contribution in reviewing and editing.

How could we get bio-fuel from forests?

The Taos News – Natural Resources Notebook. Sep 25 – Oct 1, 2008

There are two aspects of the "how to" question in using forest growth for energy: first, how to actually get bio-fuel from wood; and second, how to harvest wood in a sustainable manner.

First of all, the main reason for harvesting forest growth is for forest health. What we harvest, wood products of all sorts, can be for established uses such as lumber for building and furniture as well as potentially for energy in some form of bio-fuel. Forests continually grow so we can choose to harvest growth, at least on a portion of our public forests as part of our energy strategy as well as for traditional uses. To begin with, the technology for producing bio-fuel from cellulose, especially from wood cellulose, is in its early stages (woody tissues in trees and most plants are made up of cellulose, hemicellulose, and lignin). Cellulose is difficult to break down and requires bio-chemical processes involving enzymes. The economics are difficult to say the least, however technology is moving forward at ever accelerating rates on all fronts. For now we'll concentrate on the second aspect of energy from wood: how to harvest forest growth in the context of sustainable productive forest management. Since forest management has been around, more than a century in the US, much more in Europe, sustained yield has been an underlying principle. This means, essentially, that timber harvesting must not exceed growth in order to sustain production, basically forever, which also means without damaging forest habitat, notably soils. Nowadays, the term sustained yield has fallen out of use to accommodate a much wider principle of sustainability that, beyond production, emphasizes a wide scale of environmental as well as social aspects. Modern thinking also takes into account the fact that forests will be used for a much wider spectrum of goods and services. Public pressure has tipped the scale towards more preservation of forests and away from harvesting and production of public forests.

It's obvious that woody tissue growth cannot be taken from individual trees. It's not like harvesting fruit or nuts since the tree must be cut down. As a result, harvesting growth means first determining the rate of growth and then harvesting the number of trees whose volume is equivalent to the amount of growth. This can be done in part by thinning, but will most likely need to be complemented with full mature tree harvesting. Silvicultural systems essentially start or are based on harvesting schemes that take into consideration the ecological preferences of species, one of the most important of which is shade tolerance. Shade tolerant species tend to form uneven aged stands in which all age and size classes are present. In contrast intolerants that require full sunlight for regeneration and growth, tend to form evenly-aged stands. This is logical in that if they need full sunlight, they must all "be born" at the same time.

So determining how to harvest growth must start by recognizing the difference among forest species that make up forest ecosystems. In shade tolerant species, such as spruce-fir, and some northern and southern hardwoods it is possible to harvest individual trees under what is called a selection system. In contrast, in the case of the intolerants, harvesting must create conditions favorable for the establishment of regeneration (renewal). This means creating large open spaces, which also enhance establishment of shrubs, herbs and grasses that help diversify the forest and provide food for wildlife. This is basic forest ecology. However, in order to harvest growth, we must first determine the growth rate. How fast is a given forest growing? This is accomplished by establishing permanent sample plots, by comparing forest stands over time (also from some form of sampling) and through the development and use of mathematical and computer growth models.

Of course we would not want to subject all our public forest area to energy use. As a precaution, we could designate a small percentage limited to the least vulnerable forest stands. For example we could designate 10% of feasible forest area. "Feasible" means that the combination of slope, soil and stand characteristics is such that extractive forest management is sustainable. Environmental assessments must be done which take into to account the probable forest response to treatments.

Finally, multi-party monitoring is essential to provide a basis for adjustments in silvicultural treatments and for credibility of the public in the management process. Complete transparency is a must for any endeavor of this sort. The end result of implementing forest growth harvesting would be a healthier forest and a permanent supply of products, possibly including biofuel, and services.

Special thanks to Debbie Ragland, UNM-Taos Geology, for her valuable contribution in reviewing and editing.

ENERGY OPTIONS

In dealing with harvesting growth in a SPFM framework, forest biomass bio-fuel was an option considered. Before going into this in more depth when we will be looking at forests as huge living solar panels or leaves as tiny solar panels (all with batteries included) we'll consider a general model that could be used to deal with our nation's energy source mix.

An energy source analysis model

The Taos News – Natural Resources Notebook. Oct 23 – 29, 2008

Should we include the nuclear option as a source in developing an energy plan? If so, How much? If not, what should be the alternative sources? In what proportions?

Let's think of a way to put all our energy source options into a comprehensive and understandable condensed form in order to facilitate our political decision-making process. This is especially important at this time of hiring our next president. The idea is to develop an energy source matrix comprising all possible energy sources with their respective costs, benefits, and availability over time. A matrix is simply a table with columns and rows.

Every day there is more information on various energy plan ideas. Every source seems to have its detractors as well as its proponents. The energy source matrix would condense the proposals and vital information for each in an easy-to-understand format which would also serve to understand goals and compare the various proposals. The matrix would be made up of rows and columns. The rows would be energy sources and the columns would be specific years. The first column (column 1) would be labels identifying energy sources. The following columns could be in triplets, i.e. groups of three columns in which the first could be the total amount of each source expressed in its common unit (such as barrels for oil or tons for coal); the second column of each triplet could be a standardized unit, such as mega joules, mega-Kcal (one million kilo-calories) or a better unit to be specified; and the third in each triplet would be the percentage of total consumption. Thus the first triplet (columns 2, 3 and 4) would be our present situation. That in its self would be a major step towards understanding where we are in order to decide where we want to go. The following triplets (groups of three columns) would be for specific years which would be our goals established over time.

For example, chronological goals (our column triplets) could be set in using presidential terms: 2013, 2017, 2021, 2025 and 2029 (20 years). If we want a more extended time horizon we could jump to 2050, 2075 and 2100 after 2029. For planning purposes, the shorter presidential term periods would be good during what could be considered a transition from where we are now to where we would like to be in the year 2029, hopefully well on the road to energy independence and environmental improvement.

The first step would be to list all possible energy sources by categories in our column number 1. For example the first and most important category, based on present consumption, would of course be fossil fuels (hydrocarbons) with oil first, then natural gas followed by coal. These could be further broken down into geographical source, i.e. domestic and foreign. Foreign oil sources could be further broken down into type of transportation, i.e. pipeline for our nearest neighbors and major suppliers (Canada and Mexico) and oil tanker transport form Venezuela, Mid East and others. The rationale is both environmental and geopolitical, assuming that pipelines are safer than seagoing tankers, or at least the consequences of spills are easier to deal with over land, and that our NAFTA partners are our most reliable sources.

As we go along, our rows will get more complex since we will be considering categories and sub-categories of energy types and sources. In a fashion similar to our fossil fuel breakdown, we will have a breakdown of renewable energy sources into individual sources such as solar, wind, geothermal, tidal, biofuel, etc. We could also classify energy types by mobility. Certain types are stationary in nature, such as electricity (nuclear, coal or hydroelectric) and natural gas for homes and industry, while others are mobile, mainly as liquid fuel for cars and trucks. Trains or other electricity driven mass transportation on fixed rails or lanes with overhead wires are more stationary in nature. As with the development of any model, it tends to get more complicated as we think of additional items that we want to include. This is an undertaking that requires a team effort in order to present it to those in charge of making the decisions: the executive and legislative branches of government.

We must find a rational way to discuss alternatives and make the decisions necessary in developing a workable, "do-able" comprehensive energy strategy in which all options can be considered in the framework of a transparent, logical information model. There are no easy answers and there are trade-offs involved. Nothing is perfect.

Again, special thanks to Debbie Ragland, UNM-Taos Geology, for her valuable contribution in reviewing and editing.

An energy source analysis model: part 2

The Taos News – Natural Resources Notebook. Nov 6 – 12, 2008. p. B10

How much of our electricity consumption could we obtain from renewable sources in the short term (roughly 4 to 8 years) and in the long term (year 2029, 2050)? Of course we would like renewable energy to replace a large part of our nonrenewable fossil fuel use, but what are the do-able, realistic options? In what realistic time frame can this be accomplished? And, at what cost?

In our last article we suggested a matrix energy source / consumption analysis model in which we could organize information by source at present usage and at four-year interval goals in a matrix or table format. We also suggested classifying energy into two large groups: "stationary" (fixed in place) and mobile. Electricity would be our most common stationary energy source while the latter would refer to liquid fuels (including natural liquefied gas) used in vehicles.

Let's consider electricity in terms of sources. We should start with an estimate of over all consumption and then break it down into sources, such as nonrenewable thermoelectric (including coal, natural gas, fuel oil, and nuclear power) and renewable energy sources (including hydroelectric, solar, wind, tides, etc.). What is the total electrical energy consumption of our country and how does it break down into these various sources? Other questions which follow include how long will nonrenewable resources last and how efficient are "green" sources of energy? How detrimental to the environment are hydrocarbon-based sources? How detrimental to the environment are "green"-based sources (e.g., how many millions of square feet of solar panels would be needed to generate, say, 5% of our total consumption? How many wind turbines, as per T. Boone Pickens, for 20%?)

Potential sources of mobile energy are by nature much more restricted since the liquid fuels that we currently use in most ground transportation have to be transported within the vehicle (i.e., gasoline in cars, diesel in large trucks and trains). Solid fuels such as coal and wood are not practical (although they were used extensively in steam engine rail transportation in the 19th century). These modes of transport could eventually be fuelled by electricity (drawing on our stationary sources), but at present it is impractical and inefficient (a case in point, electric cars are still pretty much "batteries on wheels" until we have some major breakthrough in storage!). Perhaps then, in the short term we should concentrate on developing our "green", renewable energy sources for heating, cooling, and power generation in homes, businesses, and industries. This does not mean that research should not continue towards the development of alternative (hopefully, environmentally-friendly) fuels for mobile uses as, in the long term, nonrenewable sources will run out.

We have previously suggested that harvesting forest growth could provide some percentage of energy generation. Energy from wood is, after all, a reality aqui en Taos and quite an important one at that. Wood cellulose as a source of energy (with appropriate air quality protection devices) has a far greater potential in fixed non-mobile consumption than in mobile use, probably as compressed wood chips. As a mobile fuel (conversion to liquid by distillation), wood is far from an economic reality. One positive aspect of using harvested forest growth for energy production would be the potential for discounting some of the carbon emissions by crediting CO_2 taken up in forest growth (photosynthesis: sunlight to energy through plant tissue).

So, what proportion of each nonrenewable and renewable energy source do we want and how can we achieve these proportions for a long term goal, say by the year 2050, or a intermediate goal of 2025 (four presidential terms)? Our starting point is what we have now. How do we get from here to there? What are the realistic goals in terms of actually being able to achieve them considering the technical, economic and political aspects of the problem? What really is do-able? How high must the price of oil be in order for us to be able and willing to achieve our goals? Could harvesting forest growth play a significant role? Should we create an OPIC (Organization of Oil Importing Countries) and use taxes to counter oil price fluctuations in order to enhance alternatives?

We are faced with a large collection of questions all of which should be organized in a logical classification system. We would, of course, like to come up with reasonable answers. There are many uncertainties in our future, of course, such as volatile oil prices, new technological breakthroughs, varying political scenarios, legislative initiatives, and, perhaps most importantly, our desire to embrace new methods of producing and using energy. As in most cases involving natural resources, there are many trade-offs and no easy answers.

Again, special thanks to Debbie Ragland, UNM-Taos Geology, for her valuable contribution in reviewing and editing.

Developing a strategic long-range energy mix plan in the form of a matrix would appear to be an objective approach. Our renewable energy sources are a subset of the whole mix. In it we can consider the biological sources as a deeper level of our energy mix model. Biological sources can further be broken down into agricultural versus silvicultural sources. Ethanol from corn is the important element of the former. In forest biomass we have a long ways to go. A first step is more political than technological or economical. It involves getting past the "wood scrap only" source, in which the public is lead to believe that forests should not be touched other than using waste materials from construction or so-called restoration activities ("welfare forest management as it has been referred to in that it doesn't pay for itself).

Sustainable productive forest management for energy and wood products, in balance with sustainable non-extractive forest management (SNEFM) offers a huge potential for renewable energy. Just consider what the over all net annual growth (cubic feet/acre/year) of forest stands amounts to, even if only a small proportion of forests were to be put under SPFM. That's what meant by balance. Maybe a 70 / 30 (SNEFM 70% and SPFM 30%) proportion would be possible. This would depend on adequate land use planning based on topographical, geologic-edaphic (soils), forest stand, other use constraints, etc. using a GIS platform connected to math and computer projection models.

The fact that solar energy converted through photosynthesis is stored in plant tissues is what is referred to in "batteries included". The energy in wood can be harvested when needed. And when it's not need it continues to increase through growth. It's much like the principal and interest in a savings account. If we only take out the interest (forest biomass growth) and leave the principal (live forest growing stock) it is sustainable. Accounting for inflation in our model enhances economic sustainability. Taking care of the individual bank and of the banking system furthermore enhances sustainability. Likewise taking care of individual forest stands or areas of forest and the over all pool or network of forest ecosystems enhances sustainability.

Batteries included: Another angle to solar energy

The Taos News – Natural Resources Notebook. Nov 18 - 24, 2010. p. B8

Unlike most gadgets, batteries are included in our forest "green machines", which operate on solar power through photosynthesis.

Solar panels convert the sun's energy into electricity. But storing electricity is not highly efficient, yet. Everything from flashlight batteries to sophisticated computer backup power systems is relatively heavy, bulky and expensive.

However we have right before our eyes a solar energy option with batteries included. Photosynthesis is the natural mechanism that converts the sun's energy into chemical energy, basically carbohydrates, and sugars. The solar panels are leaves and pine needles (another form of leaf) in our forests (The Taos News Natural Resources Notebook, May 07-13, 2009, p B5, "Tree leaves, pine needles living solar panels?" www.cmb-lwv.com.ve/ living_solar_panels.htm). They are constantly working and are efficient. The batteries are plant tissues that store chemical energy, part of which is used to breath and to grow. The more stable form of storage, which is long term, is in the form of woody tissues made of cellulose, lignin, water and other substances. The "green machines" with their batteries included also take CO_2 out of the atmosphere, thus helping to mitigate climate change. They also make and release oxygen (O_2); all of this while providing water, outdoor enjoyment, wood products, jobs and revenue. What more of a machine could we want! Harvesting this energy source can be done under sustainable productive forest management (SPFM) on a proportion of our forests in balance with non-extractive management (preservation). An additional benefit is that it leads to a healthy forest. A further advantage is that the stored energy can be harvested when most needed since it is stored in living trees that are growing until the time to harvest.

The "batteries included" name was inspired by the film "Batteries Not Included" (a delightful film). Also, closer to the subject the "Batteries included: California passes energy storage bill" webpage. Looking up the "green machine" on the Internet shows some interesting results.

Here's an interesting hypothetical scenario. What if a group of ranchers who have diverse landscapes got together and pooled their land resources under some form of agreement. Diverse landscape means that they have range, brush, meadows, forests and high country with watersheds. They could each do land planning (zoning) within their respective ranches and a general zoning over their combined areas. The zoning could be for cattle raising, hunting, SPFM, wildlife corridors, ecotourism and watershed improvement among others. For example let's assume that together they would have an SPFM-apt area of 200,000 acres. Would that, taken as a whole, be enough to sustain some form of forest industry oriented toward energy (batteries included) and wood products? Isn't this an option that should be included in our renewable energy mix: our basket of energy sources as we reduce our dependence on oil?

Private forests are in a position to lead the way in forest biomass energy and healthy forests under SPFM. Any one ranch, especially the larger ones, is in a position to achieve a sustainable balance between non-extractive and productive forest management.

Here's a couple of acronyms: SNEFM (for sustainable non-extractive forest management) and SPFM (for sustainable productive forest management). It's fun to make up names. Then one checks them on the Internet only to find out that they have already been invented.

Batteries included: An angle to solar energy: Part 2

The Taos News – Natural Resources Notebook. Dec 09 - 15, 2010. p. B5

Can forest biomass be a significant part of our renewable energy mix?

When biomass energy is mentioned in regard to forests, the emphasis is immediately to point out that only wood scraps are involved. No tree cutting. This would give the impression that tree cutting is not acceptable. What's wrong with this impression? It is well intended but quite erroneous ecologically, economically and environmentally. There is nothing wrong per se with cutting trees. Trees within a forest are born, either survive or die early, grow and finally, just like us, die either of old age, disease, fire or insect. Individual trees are not important unless one of them happens to be your favorite shade tree in your back yard, a historical tree (like in Venezuela where there is one under which Simon Bolivar stopped to rest and is part of a monument) or other special individual trees of spiritual, historic or sentimental value. The idea of all trees being sacred is unhealthy for forests, animals and for people.

In the context of this discussion, we must differentiate between trees and forests. Obviously forests are made up of trees. What we must focus on are the forest ecosystems, not individual trees.

Regarding our public forests, among many of the owners (which means us, the people) there is strong resistance to anything having to do with timber harvesting (logging). Consequently, "sustainable productive forest management" (SPFM) is pretty much out of the question on our national and other public forests. So it would appear that it is up to private forests to lead the way and show how SPFM can be beneficial to the environment, economy and our national security (regarding not depending so much on foreign oil and with the whole out-sourcing of or economy).

In the last article ("Batteries included ...") a hypothetical scenario was described in which a group of ranchers with areas that include forests could get together and pool resources to work on SPFM in balance with conservation in general and "sustainable non-extractive forest management" (SNEFM) in particular. Extending the "what if" scenario to serve as an example, suppose that the pooled area were to be comparable to our Carson National Forest and just as diverse. In this case diversity would include crops such as alfalfa and livestock as well as natural forest, brush and meadow ecosystems. Furthermore we could assume the combined forest area suitable for SPFM to be around 20% of the total area. Could 320,000 acres of productive healthy forest be enough to support and sustain a viable forest industry with a range of green-certified wood products and energy while at the same time providing environmental services?

This would not be the first time that private enterprise would lead the way in breaking new ground. The "batteries included" renewable energy endeavor will require government involvement in funding R&D and in establishing adequate legislation and infrastructure.

We made it to the moon in an impressive one-decade stint because we decided it was worth doing. The technological, educational and economic benefits are still impacting our society. The same could be true with sustainable forest biomass energy, for many of the same reasons.

If we could get Congress to pass a "forest energy act" in a strategy involving a "forest energy initiative" similar to the Healthy Forests Initiative and the Healthy Forests Restoration Act of 2003, maybe we could set an agenda in order to explore this renewable energy option. In President Barack Obama's State of the Union address (Jan. 24, 2012), he stated that all clean renewable energy sources should be considered. Maybe we can take him up on that.

A Forest Energy Initiative

The Taos News – Natural Resources Notebook. Mar 22 – 28, 2012. p. B16

Are we ready to consider a forest energy Initiative, possibly as part of an over all energy bill? President Obama said that we should explore all sources of renewable energy in his January 24, 2012 State of the Union message. Let's take him up on it in an area that receives little or no mention.

Forests are huge solar panels that also take CO_2 from the atmosphere; provide O_2 while creating sustainable jobs that are not "outsource-able". They also provide other environmental services, such as water and recreation. This is the power of forests: growth that can be sustainably harvested for energy under productive management in balance with non-extractive preservation.

We must recognize that we have a problem regarding: energy independence; incipient renewable green energy; over-protection of forests, which leads to loss; public opinion against forest treatment involving any form of extraction; and, on top of all of these, the cost of forest treatment to improve health. A case in point: the Healthy Forest Initiative and the Healthy Forests Restoration Act of 2003, which mainly addresses fire. This is a good step forward, but remains lacking in a productive, economically sustainable effort.

In view of all of this, is it time that we gave serious thought to working on a forest energy initiative, which could develop into a component of a comprehensive energy bill? Such a congressional act could go something like this:

Whereas: 1) We have extensive and diverse areas of forests; 2) forests grow continuously with new trees being born (regeneration), growth of surviving trees and loss to mortality; 3) at some point, as a forest gets thicker, it reaches a threshold (carrying capacity) where net growth ceases; 4) overstocked (too thick) forests are prone to biomass loss to fire, insect and disease; 5) a balance between productive management and preservation can achieve true environmental, economic and socio-political sustainability; 6) harvesting forest growth on a sustainable basis to improve forest health has great potential for job creation, business opportunity enhancement and revenue building while at the same time providing sustainable environmental services, such as Carbon uptake, water, biodiversity related genetic benefits, healthy recreation and basic science; 7) a substantial productive healthy forest initiative would lead to education and R&D opportunities, benefits, comparable to the man-on-the-moon initiative of the 60's; and, finally, 8) sustainable productive forest management (SPFM) would be a major factor in energy independence and environmental sustainability.

Be it resolved: 1) that adequate resources be designated to fund a forest energy initiative proposal through a think tank; 2) that a comprehensive strategy be developed to fully explore the potential of forest ecosystems as a part of our over all renewable energy initiative; 3) that research and development efforts be enhanced in solid and liquid wood-based fuels technology; 4) that pilot-scale experimental / demonstration areas be established to gain economic and environmental knowledge, additional expertise in SPFM and in multiparty monitoring of forest ecosystem responses; 5) that existing legislation and regulations be reviewed in the context of achieving environmental, economic and sociopolitical sustainability; and 6) that a public education strategy be developed and implemented on SPFM based on sound ecological principles.

How about it?

How do we get from the forest energy initiative idea to some form of implementation? The question leads us to our next Taos News article where we explore a strategy involving pilot-scale experimental and demo sustainable productive forest management projects.

A Forest Energy Initiative Pilot Project Strategy: Part 1

Forest energy initiative pilot project. The Taos News – Natural Resources Notebook. May 31 – Jun 6, 2012. p. B12.

The idea of forests as a major source of renewable energy may seem like a radical approach to alternative energy and, as such, and at first glance, most likely will not receive much support. In order to address this issue, an approach worth considering would be to establish pilot-scale projects to further develop technical aspects of forest management practices, to serve as demonstration areas and to explore the potential for enhancing environmental services as well as social services.

The role of establishing forest energy initiative pilot projects would be to explore the integration of benefits ranging from energy and wood products to environmental or ecological services including job training, rehab and environmental education opportunities. They would be experimental in that even though there is vast experience in sustainable productive forest management over more than a century in the United States and even more in Europe, there are matters that need to be addressed, such as adequate harvest intensity regulation. A common perception that is often expressed is that during past decades our public forests were over cut; that forest service managers were too much under the influence of forest industry and that this has resulted in excessive logging that has led to over-stocked young forest stands that are now increasingly susceptible to fire. But have the areas supposedly over-harvested been objectively evaluated? It would appear not to be the case. So part of the focus of the proposed pilot projects should be on selected public forest areas that supposedly were over-cut in previous decades.

A pilot project ideally combines experimental work based on existing knowledge with innovative multiple benefit efforts that integrate environmental management and educational aspects as well as forest health. The experimental part recognizes that we don't have all the answers. The integration of a wide range of benefits leads towards enhancement of economic feasibility. A major hurdle to overcome in a forest energy initiative is the relatively low value of wood biomass. In order for wood chip energy technology to be economically viable, we need to get added value from environmental and educational benefits.

What would a forest energy initiative pilot project look like? First of all it needs to be big enough to adequately explore the economics of sustainable low value wood biomass production. On the productive side, it would include more traditional higher value wood products derived from larger trees. Adequate harvest intensity would ensure that wildlife habitat is taken into account, where actually wildlife habitat can be improved through enhanced habitat diversity, for example using a mosaic approach to stand stocking. This involves creating a "clumpy" landscape that includes open spaces, thick clumps of forest stands and everything in between.

Pilot projects would explore and further study carbon cycles in management under the premise that optimum growth leads to enhanced carbon sequestering. This is an example of an environmental service. Water would obviously be a major component.

On the educational side, pilot projects would include a wide range of educational services from job training to rehab opportunities including work camps for troubled youth. A possible focus point could be job training for vets returning from service, including any necessary rehab. Job training would range from relatively low-tech manual work to highly skilled GPS fieldwork and GIS-based planning, implementation and monitoring work.

Why not consider this?

A Forest Energy Initiative Pilot Project Strategy: Part 2

<u>Multiple benefits key to forest energy project</u>. *The Taos News – Natural Resources Notebook. Jun 14 – 20, 2012. p. B13*

The idea of a forest energy initiative involves much more than just using woody biomass for power. The key to possible long-term success resides in tying together multiple benefits, including environmental services, forest health with related reduced fire impact, jobs and education and training. The pilot project strategy involves a developmental and experimental approach to the matter.

What would such a pilot project look like? In part 1, we pointed out that it would need to be big enough to adequately explore the economics of sustainable low value woody biomass production. Over all size in area of suitable productive forest also is related to having a large enough area for adequate harvest intensity regulation. A major part of regulation is the time that is to elapse between successive harvests. In forest management this involves either rotation or cutting cycle. It is the amount of time that it takes for the forest to get to the optimum age/size and stocking density (the thickness of the forest) where an additional harvest operation is both economically viable and needed to continue to make room to grow. Keeping a forest stand within the limits of normal stocking involves successive thinning and timber harvesting operations. The interval of time between commercial harvests is the cutting cycle. Thinning and other silvicultural practices will take place during the cycle to improve productivity, forest health, economics and environmental services.

Forests are continually growing, getting thicker as existing trees grow larger and new trees are established (regeneration). Net growth rate is related to how thick the forest is, its level of stocking. As it gets thicker, above a certain threshold, growth slows down. Theoretically net growth will continually slow down until the stand reaches the carrying capacity threshold where net growth ceases.

Imagine a forest recuperating from fire. At first stocking is zero or close to it; there are no trees. As trees become established "thickness" gradually increases. At first the rate of increase, net growth, is slow. As the forest becomes thicker and occupies more of the site (soil and space, room), net growth increases.

Normal stocking is an interval of forest thickness (combination of the number of trees per acre and their size) determined by two thresholds: the first is the point at which the stand is thick enough to get maximum net growth; the second is the point at which net growth begins to decline due to overstocking (starting to get too thick).

Now back to harvest intensity regulation, the time between harvests is based on growth in trying to keep the stand within the limits of normal stocking. The slower the growth, as in our dry, short growing season climate, the longer the time between successive harvests. A cutting cycle of 100 years is manageable. So how does this affect the size of the pilot scale project? In order to explore the economics we would need fairly large annual harvest areas. The actual size will depend on many factors, one of the most important of which is the amount of usable timber in a given stand. Lets say, for example that we determine that we need an annual area of 100 acres (quite small in forestry). Then with a 100-year cutting cycle we would need a net productive forest area of 10,000 acres. If the annual area were determined to be 1000 acres, we would need a total area of 100,000 acres.

The 10,000-acre project is merely an example of how cutting cycle and annual area are related in determining over all size of such a pilot project. It is not intended as a specific proposal. In reality 100 acres is quite small and most likely a 100-year cutting cycle is too long, even for the slowest growth rates in forest stands. A more reasonable general estimate would be on the order of 50,000 acres with a 50-year cutting cycle and a 1000-acre annual area. An actual project size will obviously depend on specific conditions and economic considerations.

The idea of establishing pilot projects as a means of getting started on the implementation of a forest energy initiative involves much more than is possible to describe in the limited space of two articles. There are many aspects to consider, such as source of funding, determining economic parameters and the specifics of forest treatment in both thinning and timber harvesting.

Now we'll go back to exploring forest-related renewable energy sources.

Forests and water are closely associated and both are renewable energy sources: the former mostly potential; the latter a reality. Of course hydroelectric energy has been around for a long time and forms a significant part of our energy portfolio. However there are additional water energy options that are being explored, both in the more traditional moving water in streams and rivers though small diversified turbines and in other sources such as ocean currents.

Water and energy

<u>Water in motion is a possible energy source</u>. *The Taos News – Natural Resources Notebook. Nov 20 – 26, 2008*

Have you thought about the relationship between water and energy? Visualize a river flowing by or a waterfall and think of the energy in moving water. Of course we realize that we have hydroelectric power, the electricity generated by building dams and making the water flow through turbines to generate electricity.

Water in our area is, of course a limited resource. Our *acequias* and domestic water systems account for most of the demand. Commercial and industrial activities, such as ski resorts and mines add their share. The importance of the matter is shown by the recent Water Summit held in Taos on Nov. 5th.

Any water in motion is a possible energy source, which is the result of water getting to a higher place, like a watershed up in the mountains, and flowing down due to the force of gravity. In high school physics we learned that a rock, for example, sitting on the top of a hill has potential energy. If somehow the rock is set in motion and starts rolling down the hill, potential energy stored in the rock (just by being in a high place) is changed into kinetic energy. So water "stored" in the vegetation and soil or in a lake in a high place is potential energy. Once it's flowing we have kinetic energy that can run turbines to generate electricity or power to turn wheels to grind grain in the old grist mills.

How does the water get to a "high place"? It takes energy which, once it's used to "lift" the water, is then "stored" as potential energy. The answer: our sun's energy that drives the hydrologic (water) cycle. Water evaporates from the oceans and other bodies of water or from areas of vegetation through evapotranspiration (look up the term on your favorite web browser and you'll get over a million references), a combination of evaporation and transpiration (plants transpire –sweat- just like us), and is carried in vapor form by air currents (wind) until the mountain topography causes the moisture-laden air to rise, cool and condense in the form of rain, dew or snow. This is the process that "feeds" a watershed which acts sort of like a sponge and gradually (most of the time) releases water to feed our streams. As a result, we have water in motion which is not only good for drinking and irrigation, but is an energy source. "Most of the time" refers to watershed health and catastrophic flood events. One thing about getting energy from running water is that the water is not consumed but only slowed down transferring some of its kinetic energy into electricity as it moves the turbines. The "sponge effect" in a watershed is caused by vegetation, usually forests of various types and soil.

Watershed health is related to forest health. So: What is a healthy forest? In a nutshell, among other factors, it is one in which the total living biomass is not at or too near carrying capacity, meaning there is room to grow, which in turn means a forest that is not too thick. Vigorous growth is an attribute that improves resistance to insects and disease. "Room to grow" also means resistance to fire due to there being less fuel. We've covered the "too thick" state of a forest and what can be done about it (thinning) in previous articles.

Another situation of moving water is ocean tides. Here the driving forces are the Moon's gravity and Earth's rotation. Tidal energy offers a great potential but is still far from being a technical and especially economic reality, although there is significant ongoing research in the matter. A similar moving water situation is that related to our under-sea "rivers". Ocean currents offer a great potential that, as in the case of tidal energy, is still far from a reality and even at that, one that already has detractors. The Gulf Stream off the coast of Florida is an example. It's a dependable and essentially free source.

Now let's consider another water-related source of energy. Thermoelectric power generation that, through heat from burning fossil fuels or from nuclear reactions, uses water to convert heat (energy) to electricity. Water is heated to produce steam which drives the power generating turbines. Here water is the medium through which heat is converted to circular motion (driving the turbines) that generates electrical energy (electricity). Again, the water is not consumed in the process, but simply changes state.

Water and energy are definitely very much related, which is another reason for good water management.

Now on to another renewable source of energy: Ethanol

Ethanol: If Brazil can, why can't we?

Co-author: Dr. Debbie Ragland. The Taos News – Natural Resources Notebook. Nov 29 – Dec 25, 2007. p. C10

Over the last decade or two Brazil has made great progress in reducing its foreign fossil fuel dependence by establishing a massive program of ethanol production from sugarcane. The country is almost energy independent except for imports of natural gas from Bolivia and has announced its intention to export oil in a few years. The ethanol production program has resulted in Brazil's widespread use of fuel mixtures (85% ethanol and 15% gasoline known as alcool) and of flex-fuel vehicles. Can we in the United States realistically achieve similar results with corn, or perhaps cellulose-based ethanol and bio-waste? The answer, which is not a simple one, begins with understanding the ecology of the two crops (sugarcane and corn; we'll leave cellulose from woody plants and other bio-fuels for a later discussion), their respective producing areas, and their energy content.

One way to analyze the complexities of the bio-fuels problem is to examine the pros and cons of sugarcane and corn as fuels in terms of energy input (amount of energy used to produce the fuel) and output (energy in the fuel when we burn it in our vehicles). Energy input for bio-fuels includes energy used to grow the crop (e.g., tractors, production of seed, etc.), harvest (e.g., combines), transport (e.g., diesel trucks, trains), and conversion of the crop to ethanol (e.g., distillation). When viewed as a ratio of energy input to energy output, sugarcane has a relatively high energy output at 1:8. Corn, unfortunately, falls near the bottom of the list of bio-fuels with an input to output ratio of about 1 to 1.4. In other words, almost as much energy is used to produce corn-based ethanol as the product supplies.

Unfortunately, the United States does not have as extensive favorable growing areas for sugarcane as Brazil. Much of Brazil lies in tropical to sub-tropical climate zones whereas the United States is predominantly temperate. Our best regions for growing sugarcane are Hawaii and in the states bordering the Gulf of Mexico. Large areas of Brazil are better positioned climatically to produce bio-energy with that country's greater overall solar input and moisture availability than our temperate zones. Growing seasons in the tropics are considerably longer than those in temperate climates. Soil fertility, on the other hand, is in our favor – tropical soils are far less fertile than our rich soils in the Midwest and South. Does this offset the shorter growing seasons?

Unknowns abound in our comparison of sugarcane-based ethanol and corn-based ethanol. Does sugarcane require less cultivation than corn? Sugarcane is a perennial (comes up on its own every year) whereas corn must be replanted every year. How much energy input does this save? Does sugarcane require less fertilizers, pesticides, and herbicides? Initial studies suggest that this is true. How much CO2 is pumped into the atmosphere during distillation of these two bio-fuels? Although CO2 is removed from the atmosphere during growth of the plant, CO2 is pumped back into the atmosphere during distillation; ethanol plants use coal or natural gas in the distillation process and yeast (formed during the distillation process) produces CO2. What are the labor and capital costs? Are they lower in Brazil than the United States? How much water are we willing to sacrifice for production of ethanol? Currently, the average is four gallons of water used to make one gallon of ethanol. How much are we willing to pay in terms of lost food acreage? Every acre of crop used in the production of bio-fuel removes an acre of food from the world supply, not only taking food away from those who cannot afford it, but raising the cost to those of us who can.

The bottom line: Bio-fuels may comprise a valid alternative energy source along with other non-fossil fuels such as solar, wind, geothermal and nuclear, however, many questions must still be answered. The production of bio-fuels is an emerging technology; much more research is still required. As you can see, we do not have all of the answers. The idea of these articles is to stimulate in-depth thinking on vitally important subjects related to the preservation and remediation of our environment. These subjects are far too complex to succumb to simple answers and solutions.

By the way, ethanol is just another form of solar energy. The sun's energy is transformed to chemical energy in the form of sugars (carbohydrates) through photosynthesis aided by soil nutrients, moisture and cultivation practices. Extending the idea, way back in time, coal, oil and gas are also forms of solar energy stored in geologic formations.

What should our energy portfolio look like? We have briefly explored ethanol. How about nuclear power? To what extent should we include it?

Nuclear energy in our back yard?

The Taos News – Natural Resources Notebook. Aug 14 - 20, 2008. p. C7

Would we be more apt to accept nuclear energy if we took into account the nature of our sun's nuclear "furnace"? Also, would we be ready to consider using part of our forests' net growth for energy?

When you think of your solar panel or make sun tea, do you realize that this energy is of nuclear origin? Our sun is the main source of energy for our planet. It is, in reality, a huge nuclear plant running on atomic fusion. Yes, that's the same process as the H-bomb! And it's in our backyard! (a very large back yard some 93 million miles in radius). Our gas and diesel, propane/butane or natural gas, fuel oil, coal for our electricity and hydrocarbons for all sorts of plastics and other chemicals all came from solar energy trapped on earth by dense vegetation many millions of years ago. Present day ethanol from sugarcane in Brazil or corn in Iowa, is another form of nuclear fusion energy (sunlight) created by the process of photosynthesis in plants.

Nuclear energy comes from two types of reactions: fission and fusion. Fission is the splitting of the atom to release energy while fusion is, like it sounds, the combining atoms to release energy. So far we have not been successful in creating a process in which nuclear fusion is controlled. We have been successful in uncontrolled reactions in the H-bomb which is not a very positive track record. The Sun "controls" its nuclear fusion of hydrogen into helium through its huge gravitational force that creates a sort of high pressure oven. The sun's gigantic mass is responsible for keeping the reaction under control. When our sun, a G2 type star, starts to run out of hydrogen it will do so first in its interior, which will begin to collapse to a smaller radius before restarting the nuclear fusion fire using helium as the fuel. There will still be sufficient hydrogen in the outer layers to sustain hydrogen fusion for a while. While this is happening the energy from the interior will cause the outer shell to expand greatly and eventually engulf the orbit of the Earth. At this stage the sun will be a red giant. The inner core continues to collapse and the outer shell expands until eventually the outer shell is essentially blown off and the only the inner core is left. This small dense core, about the size of the earth, is called a white dwarf and is composed mostly of carbon and oxygen. It will continue to slowly "burn" these elements into heavier ones until it dies completely. The detailed processes of stellar evolution for our sun or any other star are a bit more complex than outlined here. However all such processes are nuclear in nature and nuclear energy is the source of energy in any star.

So could we say that since we already have a nuke in our backyard, we should be more open to nuclear energy as part of a "basket" of energy sources, at least until we find economical ways to generate large amounts of energy directly from our sun (either through solar or wind which is ultimately generated by the sun's energy)? What we're getting at here is the fact that, in addition to finding ways to conserve energy, we must consider a wide range of energy source alternatives in our quest for a better environment and energy independence. This means not putting all our eggs in one basket. We need a strategy in which all energy sources are "on the table" in varying proportions tending to substitute fossil fuels with renewable ones over time. Among the options are biological sources, (biofuels) which can come from cellulose from our forests as well as from agriculture and aquaculture (algae). Just think of the potential if we could find a way, politically as much as technically and economically, to harvest net forest growth on even a relatively small portion of our forests. It would be better than letting so much of our forest burn every year, not that we could completely prevent fires, but at least we would be able to reduce the loss through sustainably managed forests with less fuel build up and a better network of adequately built forest access roads. The idea is to get part of the forests' energy potential before nature does.

It's not going to be easy. We have some tough decisions to make which will require keeping an open mind on matters such as nuclear energy and managing forest resources for energy. We're not suggesting that forests be cut down to satisfy our hunger for energy! Again, there are no easy solutions.

Thanks to Tommy Ragland, UNM-Taos Physics, for reviewing and improving the solar scientific aspects and to Debbie Ragland, UNM Taos Geology, for her editing.

Having indulged in a very brief adventure into hydroelectric, ethanol and nuclear energy sources, we now go back to forests as a renewable energy option with great additional benefits.

SPFM, growth and energy

Sustainable Productive Forest Management

FOREST MANAGEMENT PROPOSAL

Why not take a serious look at our forests as a sustainable source of renewable energy; a source that while providing energy can do a lot more. The idea is not as someone once mentioned to cut down forests for energy. The idea is to implement SPFM on a portion of forests that would be in balance with those under sustainable non-extractive forest management (SNEFM). Timber harvesting (logging) is only a specific type of operation among many activities carried out in SPFM. The bottom line is balance, which is a key factor in sustainability.

Growth in a forest stand depends greatly on stocking levels (how thick the forest is) as well as forest type or species and habitat conditions (foresters refer to the latter as "site quality"). Growth is healthy, both for the forest itself and for the environment: the more growth, the more CO_2 that is taken from the atmosphere.

How thick is a forest and what does it mean?

The Taos News – Natural Resources Notebook. April 17 - 23, 2008. p. B11

How thick is too thick? "Too thick" means a less healthy forest where competition is excessive and susceptibility to fire, insect and disease is greater.

How do we determine if our forest is too thick (dense)? In order to develop our line of thinking we will limit ourselves to a specific area of forest: a stand. A stand can occupy a place, a site, which has finite, limited resources available, or it can be an abstract entity. A forest stand can be sparse, or open, meaning not many trees per unit of area (acre) and the trees are not too big. Or the stand can be thick or dense meaning a large number of trees of a given size or range of sizes. The easiest attribute of size to understand is bole (trunk) diameter.

We should consider two aspects of forest density ("thickness"): first, how we can describe and express it in numeric terms and second, what it means in terms of ecology and forest management. Determining total biomass would be the best method of numeric expression but it is extremely difficult to measure. Biomass is the total weight of living plant matter, which includes tree trunks (easy to measure), roots (not at all easy to measure), branches, twigs and leaves of all the trees. In addition it includes plant tissue of all other plants in the forest stand. Stocking, the number of trees per unit of area, usually an acre, can give us an approximation of density, however, problems are inherent with this method. Think about a forest stand with 100 two-inch diameter trees per acre as compared to 100 thirty-inch diameter trees. Obviously the latter is a thicker, denser forest than the former. So size is important. Consequently, we must use an expression that reflects both numbers and size.

In practical terms, foresters use more easily measured attributes of the forest stand. The most used is basal area (BA) which is the sum of the cross-sectional area of tree trunks calculated from the diameter or circumference measured at breast height (4.5 ft above the ground, termed "dbh") and which is expressed in square feet per acre. Basal area reflects both the number of trees and their average diameter (dbh) but doesn't differentiate between a lot of smaller trees or fewer bigger trees. To remedy this we use basal area in conjunction with either number of trees per acre (stocking) or average dbh. An example of BA in a fairly dense (thick) forest stand could be around 140 sq.ft./acre. This depends upon the tree species and site quality, which is the productive capacity of combined soil/topography/ and climate. 140 sq ft may be OK on a good site and too dense on a poorer site.

Now we'll consider the implications of forest density. The ecological implication is related to competition and carrying capacity of the site (the place that the stand lives on). How thick is too thick? In a forest stand that is at carrying capacity (the maximum BA that the site can support) competition is very strong and individual trees can only grow at the expense of less competitive trees, which die out to make room for growth.

The implication for management should be obvious based on the ecological considerations. If we want to grow big trees, there have to be fewer per acre so that they have room to grow. Under competitive stress, trees usually "sacrifice" diameter growth in favor of height growth in order to avoid been left behind, meaning under the shade of competitors. This is the basis for thinning, which in order to be effective must include removal of larger trees in the forest canopy. Competition is a good thing too. It helps us have straighter tree trunks (potential logs) and fewer branches on the lower portions of the trunk. It also lets us manipulate forest density in order to achieve results in diameter, which in large part determines the economy of timber production. Also the length of time required to obtain a harvest (rotation) can be manipulated to our advantage.

Regardless of whether a forest is to be used for timber production in combination with other uses or only for protection, forest health is an important consideration. Too thick means an unhealthy forest which we are more apt to lose to fire, insects (such as the bark beetle that caused so much damage to our pinyon and ponderosa pines) and disease. If a forest stand is too thick, then thin it!

Again, special thanks to Debbie Ragland, UNM-Taos Geology, for her valuable contribution in reviewing and editing.

So we see that first of all we need to know what the stocking level is (how thick it is). If we determine that it's too dense (too thick; over-stocked) then we should consider thinning as a forest treatment.

If a Forest is too thick, thin it!: Part 1

The Taos News – Natural Resources Notebook. May 8 - 14, 2008. p. C11

When a forest is so thick that it is near the site's carrying capacity, then we should thin it.

Thinning is a means through which we can regulate the density (the thickness) of a forest stand, at least in one direction. The selective removal of trees in order to reduce competition is what is referred to as thinning. A forest that is too thick is not a healthy forest and an unhealthy forest is at a greater risk of loss or damage to fire, insects or disease than a healthy forest. In our previous article, "How thick is a forest and what does it mean?" we discussed forest density and its ecological and management implications. We went over how forest health is related to forest density (how thick it is). In a forest stand whose density is near the carrying capacity, competition is excessive and tends to debilitate it. The build-up of fuel in the form of dead trunks and branches increases the intensity of a potential fire. Trees weakened by excessive competition are also more susceptible to insect damage and disease.

Thinning involves elements of science and art. The science part involves the basic knowledge and principles used in planning: how to get from the present forest stand ("here" or "now") to a desired state of the forest ("there" or "then" –the future-) which usually involves the use of math and computer models. The art element is mostly how you translate what you planned in the office on the computer to the actual selecting and marking trees for thinning on the ground in the real forest. This is a major consideration because no computer model will tell us exactly which trees should be removed. The first consideration, just like planning a trip, is to decide where you want to go with the forest. It means determining what the desired forest is supposed to be like ("there", our destination). Of course we first have to know what we want from the forest (our management objectives) and where we are to begin with ("here", our starting point), which means doing some form of evaluation to know the present state of the forest using common forestry variables such as stocking, basal area and diameter distribution. Then we need to decide how to get from "here" to "there". Assuming that we determine that it's too thick, then; we should try to thin it. "Too thick" is related to our management objectives and to the carrying capacity of the site (the physical environment or habitat meaning soil quality, topography and exposure), but in general too thick is not healthy and thus not good for any objective. What is important to consider here is that the thinning to be prescribed is objective oriented, meaning that thinning intensity will vary depending on what we want out of the forest and also on biological restrictions. Usually we will be in a multi-objective setting in which we want several things from the forest, not just one, such as timber or water. We could have timber production as a main objective with soil protection, wildlife and recreation as additional objectives. Possibly a better example would be a forest that is primarily for water production, for example, a watershed for one of our acequia systems. In this case restrictions would be imposed on other uses such as timber so that the main objective is not affected.

In order to be effective, thinning must include trees of all sizes, not just the smaller ones. If we limit our thinning to smaller undergrowth trees, we end up with a "top-heavy" forest stand in which the forest canopy is too thick. This will tend to reduce (through excessive competition, mainly for sunlight) the amount of underbrush which is important as a source of food for wildlife. Excessive competition from above (the forest canopy) also tends to leave the soil unprotected and reduces biological diversity (biodiversity) of the forest stand.

If a forest is too thick, thin it!: Part 2

The Taos News – Natural Resources Notebook – May 15 - 21, 2008. P. B13

For thinning to be effective, we need to allow the possible removal of large trees as well as smaller ones, the balance will depend on having adequate information about our forest to start with.

Before running out and marking trees for removal, it is obvious that we need a plan. We have said in our previous article that basically we need to know what the present state of the forest is, what we want our forest to be like when we're done and how to go about doing it. In planning, it is often better to start from the final destination and work back. Actually we will most likely work back and forth between the final stage (our desired forest) and the present state of our too-thick forest stand (our starting point). Of course we have to know what we have to begin with in order to define realistic objectives, so we'll start our discussion with a few ideas of how to characterize our forest in its present state. This also involves determining if our forest is really too thick. This is tricky since we probably don't know what the carrying capacity of the forest site is. What we can do is estimate the thickness by doing some sampling to have estimates of basal area (BA; total cross-section area of tree trunks per acre) and stocking (the number of trees per acre). Then we can compare our forest's values to other cases on similar sites. Finally it may boil down to deciding that since it appears that our forest is too thick, based on observation of the number of dead trees, sparseness of understory plants (herbs, grasses and shrubs), we will go ahead and thin as a precaution.

Sampling our forest involves recording the number of trees and their diameters at breast height (DBH) on plots of a given size (There are also techniques that don't require physically laying out plots). Usually it is better to have a large number of small plots rather than few large ones. The basis for this is statistical analysis and the use of sampling to have reliable information. Once we have a fairly good idea of the quantitative aspects of our present stand, we will have defined our starting point and then we can decide on what we want our future stand to be like based on estimated potential.

Typically the definition of the desired forest will include stating what the structure is intended to be. This means balancing forest density in the canopy, middle height classes and the forest floor, where herbs, grasses and shrubs will provide food for wildlife as well as cover for soil protection. Balance means that the canopy should not be too dense in order to allow resources, mainly light (solar energy), for the smaller plants. If the canopy is too thick the middle height classes and forest floor will be too sparse due to excessive shading (competition). This means that in order to get the forest we want, we have to be willing to open up the canopy to a certain extent, which in turn means removal of large trees as well as smaller ones. As we said before, taking out only smaller trees will lead to a "top-heavy" structure in detriment of shrubs, herbs and grasses as well as possible regeneration of desired tree species.

Deciding on how to get to our desired state of the forest will involve formulating a thinning regime. Usually thinning should not be considered a one-time event. That's why we use the term "thinning regime" to describe or specify a series of thinnings, each one related to the previous and following one so that they work towards the common objective. There can be several thinnings or only one, depending on the management intensity and other factors.

Due its complexity, the planning stage typically involves use of computer models to optimize the thinning regime. It requires information on forest stand structure as well as economic information on costs of operations and benefits (income) generated from the products to be obtained from the thinning. Ideally the process involves the formulation of alternatives, each of which is an option, among which we must choose. The best alternative (thinning regime) will be the one that gets us to our destination at the least cost. We also must consider the fact that thinning can be quite expensive, but the costs can be offset somewhat by income from the sale of firewood, poles or saw-timber.

Thinning is considered an intermediate treatment that is done to improve a forest stand either to make it healthier or to increase production (or both). When we have either a situation where we are at the end of the rotation in even-aged stands or the cutting cycle in uneven-aged stands, we can consider timber harvesting. Thinning also can be considered a form of harvesting when it provides useful products.

Productive sustainability involves removing timber only in the amount of stand net growth. This is like taking the interest from a savings account while leaving the principal to continue growing. Forest stand growth is the interest and the growing stock is the principal. Environmental and socio-political sustainability involves other criterion such as minimizing soil damage and assuring that environmental services and other benefits are satisfactory to the over all well-being of society.

A forest-growth harvesting model

The Taos News – Natural Resources Notebook. Dec 31, 2008 – Jan 7, 2009

Why not implement a forest growth harvesting plan, at least on a conservative precautionary scale if it meant that less than 1% (only 0.28 %) of the total would be affected each year, considering the expected benefits in terms of wood products, energy, job creation and especially forest health?

In our last article, we went over some aspects of how and where we could accomplish this. Now to further illustrate the idea, we'll assume some numbers for the sake of example.

Let's assume that we have a national forest with 1.6 million acres and that we've decided to harvest growth to provide timber, energy and jobs while at the same time improving forest health. We'll assume that most of this forest is too thick meaning that it's at or near carrying capacity. A further assumption that we'll make is that according to a hypothetical study that combines topography, soils and vegetation through overlapping mapping using a geographical information system (GIS), 20 % of the total forest area is adequate for productive management, that is, timber harvesting and thinning. This would be an area of 320,000 acres (20% of 1,600,000 acres), which we would designate as potential productive forest. Now, in order to further establish a balance between preserved area and productively managed area, we will decide to set aside 30% of the 320,000, an area of 96,000 acres, which will be done using mapping techniques so as to include representation of all major types of forest. This will also serve as a basis for comparison between untouched forest and treated forest. "Treated" means a combination of timber harvesting and silvicultural practices. As a result, our net productive forest area is 224,000 acres (320,000 minus 96,000).

Our next step is to assume a cutting cycle of 50 years, which is the number of years between successive harvests. This allows time for the forest ecosystem to respond to our treatment. We divide the net productive area of 224,000 acres by 50 in order to establish an annual area of 4,480 acres in which a group selection silvicultural system will be applied. We assume the main species to be partly intolerant to shade, for example Ponderosa pine, in which groups of trees are marked for removal making small gaps in the forest which serve to create conditions for regeneration of the pine as well as maintaining or even increasing biodiversity and providing food for wildlife.

Since our underlying principle is sustainably harvesting forest growth, we must determine how fast the forest is growing or rather would grow if the stocking level were more adequate (some point below carrying capacity). For the purpose of our model we'll assume an over all average growth rate of 5 cubic feet per acre per year. Actual growth rate can be estimated through various means, using forest mensuration (measuring) tools such as permanent growth plots and tree ring studies. At the rate of 5 cu.ft./acre/year, the net productive forest area of 224,000 acres would have a total annual growth of 1,120,000 cu.ft. Therefore, we would harvest this same volume every year but only on our annual area. We wouldn't want to go over the whole area every year just picking out groups of trees. That would be disorderly, costly, and most important, not good for the forest considering the moving around of logging equipment, the need to build all the roads at once and so on. That is why we set up annual management areas (compartments) in which we will concentrate timber harvesting, thinning and silvicultural measures that may include planting seedlings in the gaps created by our harvesting. Therefore we will carry out these activities on the 4,480-acre compartment, which for practical and economic reasons we would probably want to divide into smaller more manageable units, for example, ten 448-acre units to handle every year.

Now we'll see how this breaks down in terms of the number of trees and volume per acre over the annual compartment. The average volume per acre that we will remove in our harvesting (logging) would be 250 cu.ft. / acre (1,120,000 cu ft divided by 4,480 acres in the annual compartment). Assuming that the average tree has a volume of 10 cu.ft, we'll harvest an average of 25 trees/acre out of, say, an average of 120 per acre in the forest stand before treatment. This amounts to a 21% removal proportion on a given stand. The over all proportion of forest treatment would be 0.28 % each year and 14% over the whole 50-year rotation, leaving 86% of the total forest untouched.

We must also assure skeptics that road building and logging procedures will be done according to specifications that will minimize the impact and that all other uses of the forest will be accommodated. In the end public multi-party monitoring will ensure that the whole operation is supervised and that all information is available to the public. Environmental groups will be encouraged to take part in all steps of planning, implementation and monitoring of outcomes. As we can see, the progress of operations will be gradual which will allow for corrections as we move from each annual compartment to the next. It will take us 50 years to cover the whole area of the net productive forest, so there is time to make adjustments based on the follow-up monitoring of the forest ecosystems' response to our treatments. The economics of the whole endeavor is another aspect to consider.

Is there really any good reason not to try it?

Again, special thanks to Debbie Ragland, UNM-Taos Geology, for her valuable contribution in reviewing and editing.

More on how to harvest forest growth – the economics

The Taos News – Natural Resources Notebook. Jan 22 -28, 2009. p. C5

Is making a profit a bad thing in forest management? If we decide to go ahead and try to harvest forest growth on a public forest, such as the Carson National Forest, for timber (lumber), energy and to improve forest health, how much would it cost? Who would pay for it? If the Forest Service were to do all the work, it would be the taxpayers. It could be said that the forest has a good amount of capital in standing timber that can pay for most if not all of the growth harvesting treatment (management). We must remember that sustainability is not only in terms of the environment, but also in economic and social terms. If a management endeavor pays for itself as well as being based on sound ecological principles and is supported by the public (the social element), it is more likely to be sustainable in the long run.

We have established in previous articles that in order to improve health in a forest that is at, or too near, carrying capacity, we must reduce the stocking level by removing trees. If the forest stand largely is made up of relatively big trees, just thinning smaller trees won't make much difference. Removal of large trees, say DBH greater than 15 or 18 inches, is logging and involves the techniques, methods, benefits and dangers inherent to it. Large tree removal (harvesting) is expensive but the value of the timber / lumber, plywood, veneer can provide the income to cover costs and most likely make a profit.

Profit is a driving force our economy. I have heard from some individuals something to the effect of "Thinning even larger trees would be OK just as long as somebody, or especially some company, isn't making a profit off of it". So we're back to our initial question: Is making a profit bad in forest management? If one were to answer "yes" then we must ask a follow-up question: Why is making a profit in forest management different from any other business activity? Are forests sacred? Some are for sure and we wouldn't want to touch them, but they're an exception.

Someone might say, well, OK a profit, but not too much. Another question: How much is "too much"? Here we get into some pretty heavy ideological matters. OK profit is good as long as it's not excessive. Who determines what is too much or excessive? And how? Using what parameters?

How is farming different from productive forest management? Would we expect our farmers and ranchers to produce food for us without making a profit? What is the difference between harvesting wheat and harvesting wood? If it has to do with killing trees, wheat plants are just as much living things as trees. Would those opposed to harvesting trees also oppose harvesting (killing) wheat plants? Again, the problem is where to draw the line. Where do we draw the line between reasonable monetary motivation (incentive, profit, money-making) and greed (too much profit)? As in many cases, we can identify the extremes (according to our own values) but have difficulty dealing with differentiating (drawing the line) when things are on a continuous gradient, like from "rich" to "poor".

The basic, underlying matter is sustainability. Of course we should not support harvesting trees if it's not sustainable. But forests grow whether we like it or not. And through the sum growth of all the individual trees, they get thicker and thicker until they reach carrying capacity of the site where competition is fierce and health declines. Then something happens to change that. In nature that "something" is fire, disease or insects (such as mountain pine beetle – bark beetle) or even wind.

In managing public forests, profit-making is not an object. The policy, objectives and goals of the over all sustainable forest management endeavor are oriented towards maximizing public benefit which means all uses of forest ecosystems, ranging from protecting without planned alteration to intensive productive forest management. However, specific operations, such as harvesting (logging) can pay their own way and probably produce a positive margin for the public (a profit? Meaning more income to the Forest Service than expenses) in view of the fact that standing timber (stumpage) is valuable to society, which in turn means that society consumers will pay a fair?? price which will cover logging and milling costs and leave some over as incentive to the entities (logging companies and their workers) and even pay some of the forest management costs.

There are other sources of revenue from the sort of forest management endeavor proposed here. An actively growing healthy forest should sequester more Carbon (CO_2) than an over-stocked, too thick forest. This could lead to carbon credits. Even if the harvested wood were for energy, at least it would be "carbon-neutral". Furthermore, concerning energy, there is a strategic value as well in working towards energy independence by replacing foreign oil.

The bottom line: Why not give this a try?

Forest management for change: Part 1

The Taos News – Natural Resources Notebook. Feb 5 – 11, 2009. p. B7

With change taking place in our national administration, having gone through the process of hiring our new national CEO and a good part of congress to go along with him, could part of that change be in the form of re-thinking our public forest management policies, objectives and strategies?

We've been developing a forest management strategy proposal in previous articles in which forest growth could be harvested for a combination of wood products and energy while at the same time improving forest health. Now we'll consolidate the main elements of the idea and add a few more. Much of the forest management endeavor can most likely be paid for (financed) by the forest capital that's on the stump, meaning standing timber of commercial value.

Taos County and North Central New Mexico in general very badly need a comprehensive land and water use strategy, much of which is in the process of being put in place with significant efforts in striving for sustainability. We are at risk of losing water through water rights transfers and especially land use patterns that take place through a natural process of land subdivision, not only by developers, but also by families that traditionally have used the land who, for the last couple of generations, are providing for new generation family needs by dividing up the land among children and grandchildren.

A land-use planning model would consider the dominant uses: residential, agricultural, tourism, mining and (very little) productive forest management. All of these are important. With more and more people moving to our area to enjoy the natural beauty and culture, residential use is probably becoming the dominant income and revenue-generating land use. Tourism in all its forms and seasons is also a major use. Mining is limited to one large scale operation and a few smaller ones mostly in sand and gravel. Productive forest management is practically non-existent, while agriculture is struggling to survive. Land-use planning must accommodate all these and other uses in a sustainable manner. The key is striking a balance. In agriculture we need one or more highly productive activities to replace alfalfa producing which has a short economic chain meaning it doesn't have much potential to generate jobs and business opportunities. Perhaps a subsidized (sounds like pre-bailout?) biofuel program would be a possibility where the growing of canola or other crops and the associated processing would lengthen the economic chain. Our limitations in water and growing season are severe but not insurmountable.

Productive forest management, where "productive" means mainly, but not exclusively, use for wood products, is one of the economic activities with the longest chain of benefits. This means that from forest management in the woods all the way to the final consumer, there are multiple "links", each of which offer job and business opportunities for a entities ranging from the small family business to sophisticated and capital-intensive enterprises. Examples of the former are low capital requirement activities such as marking boundaries, building trails, small-wood harvesting (small poles, latillas, wood for traditional and pellet industry use). "Low capital requirement" might mean a truck, chainsaws, hand tools and a desire to work. Arranging financing for them should not be a problem, which could be readily do-able for local banks. On the high end of the capital investment scale we could have product-integrated wood processing mills for a wide range of products, including relatively low tech (wood pellets, compressed sawdust) and high tech wood products and cutting edge (such as wood distillation for liquid fuel – not yet an economic reality) energy alternatives.

The benefits in terms of wood products, energy, job opportunities and forest health should outweigh the costs in terms of the probable need for substantial subsidies. Is there really any reason not to go ahead on this, proceed to the economic evaluation and finally to the implementation of such a forest management model? Particularly, is there any reason to oppose it on supposedly environmental grounds when an appropriate scale can be implemented and multi-party planning and monitoring can be put in place for public scrutiny? Striking an appropriate sustainable balance between using and preserving our public forests is not such a difficult thing to understand, consider and support. Why not do it?

Forest management for change: Part 2

The Taos News – Natural Resources Notebook. Feb 19 – 25, 2009. p. B5"

Can a small proportion of our forests be managed in such a way as to help alleviate our economic situation by creating jobs, while improving forest health by making room to grow and reducing fuel for fires and at the same time providing a source of renewable energy? Yes it can.

The last few articles have been on developing a forest management proposal in the context of sustainably harvesting forest growth for improving forest health, for wood products, for energy and for jobs. The underlying principles for this proposal are: 1) a healthy forest is one in which there is room to grow meaning not too thick; 2) growth can be harvested in a sustainable manner using existing forest management technology; 3) harvesting, in the framework of integral forest management, can be done on a relatively small scale, involving less than 1% of total forest area on any given national forest, through planning that involves selecting appropriate forest areas in terms of topography (slope), soils and forest stand characteristics; and 4) forest ecosystems are fundamentally resilient meaning that they tend to recover from alterations of various degrees whether human-made or natural.

The elements of the proposal can be summarized as follows: 1) formulation of detailed forest management plans based on forest conditions in which thinning and timber harvesting are to be carried out under a set of rigorously established specifications based on sound forest ecology, silvicultural and economic principles; 2) selection / designation of pilot priority treatment areas which are most suitable for productive forest management by combining (overlapping) topographic, soils and forest stand information; 3) use of optimal growth under managed conditions (keeping the forest from being too thick, maintaining room to grow) as a criterion for setting harvest intensity, i.e. the proportion of standing timber to be removed at a given time and the frequency of such removal (the cutting cycle).

The proportion of standing timber to be removed at a given time and the cutting cycle (frequency of harvesting) are like two levers that can be used to regulate harvesting intensity. They can be set conservatively in order to achieve the goal of sustainability. For example the proportion to remove at a given time can be set relatively low, say 10% of the standing biomass. This harvest intensity can be repeated on a long cycle, say 50 years, to allow sufficient time for the forest ecosystem to respond. It also can be adjusted on the basis of information obtained through monitoring. Such long cutting cycles are possible where we have large areas of forest, since the annual area (acres/year) is calculated by dividing the net productive management area by the cutting cycle. Response can be measured in terms of growth, degree of biodiversity (including wildlife habitat), water quantity and quality if it's part of a watershed, the degree to which recreational activities can be maintained, or any other criteria that would be established in the management objectives.

What are the risks or the expectations in terms of sustainability? First, regarding environmental sustainability, achieving the goal is assured based on: 1) The cumulative knowledge available on forest ecosystems in terms of growth and their response to treatment. 2) The fact that the proportion of forest area to be treated (net productive management area) can be kept low as developed in "A forest-growth harvesting model" (The Taos News Jan 8th or 15th), in which in only 224,000 acres would actually be treated on a 1.6 million acre forest, after determining that only 20% is suitable (320,000 acres based on topography and forest stand characteristics) and that 30% of this area

(96,000 acres) would be set aside. The net 224,000 acres would be treated over a 50-year period (our cutting cycle), i.e. an annual area of 4480 acres, which only amounts to 0.28% of the total area. As a result, by the 50th year, only 14% of total area will have been treated and the first 4480 acres will have had 50 years to respond without further alteration. The rest of the forest (86%, 1,376,000 acres) will remain unaltered except for natural causes such as fire or bark beetle. 3) The short-term and long-term outcomes would be closely monitored by management and by external parties, meaning the general public through various non-governmental organizations.

Second, regarding technical sustainability, the technology for sustainable forest management exists as a result of management efforts from a century of experience based on: 1) growth data; 2) data on silvicultural practices and techniques; and 3) timber harvesting engineering methods that comply with restrictions to mitigate impact regarding road design and construction and logging techniques.

Third, regarding economic sustainability, the risks are higher in that there is need to study costs and benefits, especially in relation to energy. This is probably the area in which the most study is going to be required in order to turn this proposal into a doable project. In contrast to bailouts, this can be made to be a sustainable endeavor in the long run as well as short term.

Fourth, social sustainability is also a problem area, mostly regarding how the general public feels about productive forest management. It will take great effort to educate the public on forest ecology and management, which, if successful, should turn into positive pressure on politicians in the executive and legislative branches of government at all levels.

Yes we can.

In the process of harvesting growth under SPFM, we end up with a healthier forest, meaning one with room to grow, diversity, low dead fuel and healthy soil. So next, we consider what a healthy forest is (or as one of my UNM-Taos Forest Ecology students put it, What is not a "crappy forest"?)

Are not all forests green?

The Taos News – Natural Resources Notebook. April 23-29, 2009. p. B6

We have buildings and we have green buildings. We have energy and we have green energy. Could we say that we have forests and we have green forests? Are not all forests green?

We could say that a "green forest" is a healthy forest. It's a forest that is growing at or near the greatest growth rate possible for the combination of habitat (in forestry terms, the "site" referring to "site quality", mostly forest soil) and forest community. It's a forest ecosystem in which there is room to grow with not too many open spaces, but just enough, nor too few trees but just enough.

Why is this forest green? The answer is that, because it's growing vigorously, it's "soaking up" the maximum amount possible of carbon dioxide (CO2) from the atmosphere, thus helping to offset carbon emissions from our energy-using habits that most probably are contributing to climate change: global warming. So a green forest is better at carbon sequestering (carbon "fixation": taking Carbon out of the atmosphere and turning it into carbohydrates, food, and woody tissue) than a not-so-green forest. More growth, as well as healthy, means that more CO_2 is taken out of the atmosphere.

To maintain room to grow, trees must be removed periodically from the forest. (Nature only does this when the forest is too thick.) This means some form of thinning in which not only small trees are removed but also large ones. This is to make room for growth "up in the forest canopy" and at the same time maintain a structural balance. "Structural" has to do with the proportions of large, medium and small trees, a form of diversity, which, along with biological diversity, is a major factor in forest ecosystem health.

Conversely a not-so-green forest is one that is too thick meaning it has little or no room to grow. If it does not grow (little or no net growth) then it is not taking up carbon (in terms of net change). It's only storing it. It also means that not being so healthy, it's more susceptible to insect, disease and fire.

Now here are some additional benefits of such a green forest. Making and maintaining room to grow, thinning, also gives us forest products, including energy, and in doing so, generates economic activity, hence jobs. This is an economic stimulus that will not be totally paid for by taxpayers. Why? Because the forest products have value which will at least pay for part of the whole operation and part of the over all management costs. What we are referring to is sustainable "productive" forest management, where "productive" means that management is mainly, but not exclusively for production. Such a productive forest can form a buffer zone around forests that we want to remain protected (preserved) resulting in a balance between "productively" managed forests and those managed for preservation.

A final thought. Tree leaves and pine needles could be considered miniature solar panels and very special ones at that. Why? Because, as they capture solar energy to make "food" in the form of carbohydrates (another form of energy through photosynthesis), they are also removing a greenhouse gas (CO_2) from the atmosphere. We can "harvest" their Carbon in the form of wood, which we can "store" in wood products in buildings, furniture and artwork or use as energy.

Tree leaves, pine needles living solar panels?

The Taos News – Natural Resources Notebook. May 07-13, 2009. p. B5

Tree leaves and pine needles are like miniature solar panels and very special ones at that. Why? Because as they capture solar energy to make "food" through photosynthesis, they also remove an important greenhouse gas, carbon dioxide (CO_2), from the atmosphere.

Imagine the number of such solar panels in any one of out Taos area forests. They come in quite a range of sizes and shapes. There are two major categories: leaves and needles. Their "owners" and "managers" (the trees) are able to arrange them so that they make the best use of solar energy reaching the forest. This depends in part on forest structure: the diversity in tree size and spatial distribution and also on how thick the forest is.

What do they do with the product of their efforts? The "product" is, in general, a group of carbohydrates (mainly various forms of sugars) that they make from CO_2 and water by means of the chloroplasts in their very specialized cells using the sun's energy and forest soil nutrients such as nitrogen, phosphorous and potassium. They use the carbohydrates that they make to build plant tissue to replace worn tissues and to grow new ones. Plant tissues, mostly cellulose and lignin, make up branches, twigs, roots and tree-trunk wood, which support the whole food "factory apparatus" which is the whole network of leaves. Woody tissues provide lumber for furniture, homes and art and firewood and other forms of energy that we can use in a sustainable way.

And while they're doing this, they are soaking up carbon CO_2 from the atmosphere, working hard to offset all the same stuff that we are putting into it driving our SUV's, running our coal-driven electricity plants and, yes, even our breathing. In doing so they "produce" oxygen for us and most other living things.

The faster the forest is growing, the more CO_2 it takes out of the atmosphere. If we decide to do it, we can make certain areas of forest grow faster and increase the rate of carbon fixation. The manner in which we can do this is by making and maintaining room to grow. Through thinning and timber harvesting we can keep the forest ecosystem biomass lower than the habitat's carrying capacity creating growing room and making the forest healthier.

Once we have a healthy growing forest, we can put in place a system of harvesting growth. The rate of wood product removal from the forest would not exceed growth. This is somewhat like "harvesting" the interest of a savings account without touching the principal. This is one of the principles of sustainable productive forest management. We can make provisions to maintain a balance between the areas of forest managed for production with areas of forest managed for preservation. One way to do this is to create buffers zones of treated forest around areas that we want to preserve, like wilderness areas.

If our politicians, with our support, put some form of carbon tax and carbon credit system in place, our faster-growing forests could also generate income that can be used to pay for management. In addition we can have wood products, including energy, which can act as a stimulus package: jobs (at little or no taxpayer cost).

A healthy forest is one that is growing and in doing so helps mitigate our greenhouse-gas climate change, produces wood, energy and oxygen and, in the process, jobs.

Forest treatment and soil health

The Taos News – Natural Resources Notebook. April 9 - 15, 2009. p. B9

Do roads endanger a forest ecosystem?

The greatest threat to forest soil health is erosion beyond that which is normal. Erosion is a natural process and is part of forest ecosystem dynamics which means that a certain degree of soil erosion is taking place as an unaltered forest is ever changing through natural processes of growth, regeneration, mortality and natural events involving fire, insects and disease. Removal of trees in thinning or mature timber harvesting can improve forest health in maintaining room to grow and lower levels of fuel for fire. Furthermore, adequately planned removal can actually enhance biological diversity by improving stand structure and creating open spaces that provide habitat for other types of plants such as shrubs, grasses and herbs. Thinning and timber harvesting are parts of an over all management strategy and should not be considered separately. They provide forest products, including the potential for energy beyond our traditional use of firewood while at the same time providing for better forest health and providing jobs. Obviously roads are needed to get the products from the forest to processing mills.

A concern to be addressed is how thinning and timber harvesting affect forest soil health. Log skidding and road building for hauling have an impact on soils. However adequate road network design is possible and is a must for forest management sustainability. Roads can be designed in such a way as to have minimal impact on forest soils and the forest ecosystems in general. Road density is a major factor. There is a trade-off between road density (miles of road per square mile of forest area) and skidding distances. Having fewer roads means having longer skidding distances from the stump to the loading site. Conversely, having a greater road density results in shorter skidding distances. Skid trails can also be optimized taking into account timber density and slope, as well as costs per mile of skidding. The alternative is where topographic conditions, mainly slope, allow loading at the stump, meaning you drive a truck up to or near each tree. It can be argued that the latter has a greater impact than optimized skidding. Optimization is based on loading site locations, skidding distances and road density and takes into account slope restrictions, special soil conditions (such as wet areas). This is an example of how restrictions are put in place on an activity in order to make it compatible with other uses and sustainability in general.

Forest soil health and sustainability of productive (extractive) management practices can be accomplished through adequate road-building specifications. Some examples are: implementing maximum slope (meaning, for example, using contours in road layout), providing for effective use of culverts and water diversion ditches along roadsides and good maintenance.

Adequate multi-party monitoring is a must as follow-up of the whole process of thinning and timber harvesting. Roads and skid trails must be inspected periodically to detect any sign of above-normal erosion. This should provide for public credibility while at the same time provide information that can be used to improve future practices.

Concern about road and other impacts of productive forest management should not be a reason to not proceed in using a small part of our public forests to further benefit society.

An efficient and sustainable road network provides the infrastructure for approaching the matter of healthy forest stocking. Achieving the just right, not too thick and not too sparse, stocking level is done by periodic removal of forest biomass through thinning and timber harvesting. This can be seen as a means of optimizing the forest living solar panel array.

Forest density and structure determine "living solar panel" efficiency

The Taos News – Natural Resources Notebook. May 21-27, 2009. p. B1

Can our forest "living solar panel array" made up of leaves and pine needles be made more efficient? Think of forest "structure" and "thickness" and how it can be manipulated.

Our forest ecosystem living solar panel's efficiency depends on forest stocking (density, "thickness") and structure (tree size and spatial distribution). Forests "manage" their "solar panel arrays" in such a manner as to make the best use of the resources at hand. The main resources are sunlight (solar radiation that reaches the Earth's surface is made up of more than visible light), water, space to occupy and grow in and soil nutrients. The "array" is supported by a complex network of woody tissue in the form of tree trunks (the main support platform) branches and twigs that we can see, and complex root systems that we can't see.

A further complexity is the intense interaction among the individual components of the "array": the trees. Trees and other plants compete for resources in their habitat. The most visible object of competition is sunlight. Trees are constantly trying to gain and maintain a competitive advantage in their quest for energy (kind of like us) in the forest environment. Over long periods of time, through natural selection (survival of the fittest), they have perfected a wide range of competitive strategies. Some (the shade intolerants) grow fast to get above the rest; some tolerate shade to various degrees so that they can regenerate and survive without having to grow faster and taller than others nor to need open spaces; others have unique leaf shape patterns and arrangements that allow for great energy absorbing efficiency as is the case of the conifers which have needle-shaped leaves such as our pines, firs and spruces. Shade tolerance is a major factor in forest ecosystem dynamics.

Forest "thickness", stocking, is the amount of total biomass (the sum weight of all living things) relative to the carrying capacity of the site (habitat: combination of climate, micro-climate, soil). A forest whose biomass is at or near the limit has little or no "room to grow"; growth is limited to woody tissue replacement with very little (or no) new woody tissue biomass added to the system.

Before making any decision on treating the forest through wood/ timber removal, we must get to know the forest through some form of sampling. The most useful data to be taken is stem diameter measured at 4.5 feet above ground (DBH). It's a measure of the size of the tree in terms of its trunk. From the set of tree trunk diameters of trees on each sample plot, we can get the stand density (number of trees per acre), basal area (the sum of the cross-sectional areas of tree-trunks: an approximation to thickness or stocking level) and diameter distribution. Diameter distribution by size classes gives us a good idea of the vertical structure of the forest stand. Remote sensing, using satellite images or aerial photographs, can give provide information on spatial distribution, especially regarding open spaces of various sizes which enhance diversity.

With the resulting information expressed in terms of statistics that tell us how good our estimates are, we can determine whether a forest requires treatment and if so, how it should be done. Part 2 will further develop the idea of forest treatment to improve the forest solar panel array's efficiency.

Forest treatment can improve "living solar panel" efficiency (Part-2)

The Taos News – Natural Resources Notebook. May 28 - June 3, 2009. p. B13

How can forest "structure" and "thickness" be modified to make our forest "living solar panel array" more efficient? The emphasis here is on describing a given forest stand as the basis for planning whether or not to apply some form of silvicultural treatment and if it's to be done, then how to determine its intensity. First we have an adequate diagnosis, and then we proceed to prescribe treatment.

Before we go any further on the topic it's important to understand that a balance is needed between preserved forests and productive forests. The balance can be in terms of general proportions. It will be necessary to determine which areas of forest are for what. It is also good to bear in mind that productive forest areas can be made to provide a buffer around protected areas.

Ideally, a silvicultural treatment such as thinning should not have any pre-determined restrictions that are not related to actual forest stand conditions. A case in point: a 12-inch diameter maximum on tree removal in thinning (as reported for a local thinning project). Any treatment is based on a diagnosis and not a pre-determined standard procedure of some sort. Imagine if doctors worked under a regulation that in no case is an organ to be removed! Any such unrealistic "regulation" would only make health matters worse. Well, the same is true for a forest stand, which presents a certain set of forest conditions that may or may not be considered a "disease" or health problem. If a forest is too thick, then it must be diagnosed to determine the best remedy. The "best" will depend on the nature of the unhealthy situation.

First, as part of our diagnosis, we'll consider the "thickness" aspect referred to as stocking level. Stocking is a term used by foresters to express the wood biomass, usually limited to tree trunk volume per acre. Volume would be a good variable but it's difficult and costly to determine.

Basal area (BA) is used as a shortcut estimator of volume and in general of stocking level and only requires measurement of diameter measured at breast height (4.5 feet; DBH), which is easy to measure. BA is the sum of the cross-sectional areas of tree trunks. However, among other limitations, BA does not differentiate between a large number of small trees and a small number of large trees. To do this, foresters use an expression of stand density, which is simply the number of trees per acre. Combining the two gives an expression of stocking level and average size of trees in the forest stand.

Biological, vertical (structural) and spatial diversity is important in prescribing stand treatment. Diversity leads to stability through resilience (the capacity of a forest ecosystem to recover from alterations). Structural diversity means there is a healthy variation in trees sizes in the stand. Again height would be a good variable to use but it is costly. So foresters tend to use DBH. A useful expression is diameter distribution or stand table that tells how the trees are distributed in DBH size classes.

Next we'll go into more detail on diagnosis and treatment in sustainable productive forest management, keeping in mind that management for production and for preservation must be kept in balance.

Forest diagnosis and treatment to improve density, structure

The Taos News – Natural Resources Notebook. June 11-17, 2009. p. B5

Prescribing forest treatment to improve "structure" and "thickness" to make our forest "living solar panel array" more efficient is a planning process.

A forest treatment plan, like any other plan, should be based on a diagnosis. In this part, we'll go into how foresters do the diagnosis and how the treatment is prescribed in sustainable productive forest management. But first, we'll remind ourselves that a balance is needed between preserved forests and productive forests and that the latter can provide a buffer around protected areas. Formulation of pilot projects would be a good way to get started.

Diagnosing a forest stand's condition involves data gathering and processing to provide information pertinent to the decisions that need to be made. The first decision is whether or not the stand needs treatment.

Is the forest "sick"? Once it's determined that it needs treatment, the next decisions involve how to go about doing it which obviously depends on its specific conditions. The main descriptive variables used are: basal area (BA), average bole diameter (DBH) and diameter distribution. BA is an expression of "thickness" which we can refer to as stocking. "Too thick" means that the BA of the stand is too high, too close to the carrying capacity leaving too little room to grow. An additional variable is age, which can be determined in our temperate forests by increment bores in which annual rings can be identified and counted.

A sample composed of a series of plots can be taken in order to get meaningful values of BA, average DBH, diameter distribution and age. Statistical analysis is used to determine how well the sample results describe the actual forest stand conditions. In decision-making, it's important to know how reliable the sample information is, on which the treatment will be based.

Including age in sampling, along with previous knowledge of the forest stands, allows foresters to determine what kind of stand it is. Basically there are two general types of forest stands: even-aged and uneven-aged (all-aged) stands. An even-aged stand, as the name implies, is one in which all or most of the trees are roughly the same age, which means that they probably got established as a result of some form of disturbance, such as fire. This also implies that the trees do not tolerate shade. In contrast, an uneven-aged stand implies that regeneration (new trees being born) is a continuous process and that the trees are shade tolerant (this doesn't mean that they like shade). Treatment should be prescribed accordingly. In general, in young even-aged stands, thinning through removal of mostly small trees is the likely treatment. In older, mature, even-aged stands, timber harvesting is the likely treatment in the form of clear-cutting using relatively small patches in a sustainable framework. In uneven-aged stands, the most likely treatment is a form of selection cutting of some mature trees and some thinning of smaller trees. Here diameter distribution is important. It can be used to balance the tree removal process.

The bottom line: Forest treatment is prescribed on the basis of reliable information obtained through objective sampling and not on pre-conceived regulatory specifications, such a 12-inch diameter maximum on tree removal or precluding clear-cutting as a valid silvicultural practice in sustainable forest management.

FOREST TREATMENT: RESTORATION – RESTORE TO WHAT?

The term forest restoration is commonly used to refer to treatment usually involving thinning with logging not an option; it's not politically correct. The following series of four articles published from December 2010 to March 2011 addresses this matter. The bottom line: treatment is objective oriented. It means going from "place" A, the initial forest stand conditions (most likely too thick with too much fuel), to "place" B, the desired forest stand conditions, i.e. healthy forest. Instead of restoration we should consider SPFM. (Remember? Sustainable productive forest management, which should be in balance with SNEFM – preservation.)

Forest treatment: Restore to what? Part 1

The Taos News – Natural Resources Notebook. Jan 6 - 12, 2011. p. B7

We use the term "restore" in many ways regarding our natural resources. The term implies that we go back to a desirable situation like restoring a deteriorated historic building to its original state.

So what is meant by forest restoration? A common use today is with regard to forest treatment to reduce fuel. Thinning, which involves cutting live trees, and removing dead fuel (tree trunks and branches) help make the forest healthier and more resistant to fire, insect and disease. A healthy forest can be considered one in which: 1) there is room to grow; 2) there is biological, spatial (habitat) and structural (tree size) diversity; 3) an adequately low level of dead fuel; and 4) healthy soil.

In recent years we've experienced quite an intensive outbreak of bark beetle in our pinyon pine forests. It was especially intense during the years of drought and the effects can still be observed, though most of the dead trees are now decaying and falling down. First they turned brown, then gray. The insects are in the trees all the time but only do "damage" when trees are under stress. Drought is a major cause of such stress, which theoretically is greater under more severe competition for moisture. The degree of competition is directly related to stand stocking: how thick the forest is. In a forest that is too thick, competition is greater, thus stress is greater, especially when moisture is more scare than usual.

Forest treatment involves thinning to reducing the stocking level of the forests, making them less "thick" providing room to grow and "fuel management" through physical removal or prescribed burning. Growth is healthy. Growing trees are more vigorous and more able to survive disease and insects such as the bark beetle. Having fewer trees die means less dead fuel and consequently less fire occurrence and/or intensity and rate of spread.

The more obvious objective of treatment is to lessen the risk of fires spreading. Fires occur mostly due to human actions but also due to lightning. Once a fire occurs, the rate of spread will depend on many factors that interact. The amount and condition of fuel is a major one. Other factors are wind, relative humidity, fuel moisture content, etc.

At present, work is being done to reduce fuel in the wildland urban interface WUI, pronounced wooie (rhymes with Louie). Relatively small areas of the extensive WUI forest areas are being treated at a fairly high cost. Thinning and removal of dead wood is costly. When there is no market for what is removed, the work is paid for by taxpayers ("welfare forestry"?).

The term restoration is not appropriate for this kind of forest treatment. Nature restores by fire, insect and disease, often combined. A forest that is too thick is eventually replaced by new plant communities (ecological succession). After an intense fire, nature responds with grass, brush, and over time back to trees again. If we go in and thin out the forest, it is less likely to burn, or at least less likely to burn as intense as if it were not treated. But is this restoration?

We should clearly define what we mean by restoration. Or else it's like not knowing where we're going. Maybe "Restore," sounds good. It's probably a lot more palatable than "logging" to many people. It's a case of semantics.

Best wishes to all for a great 2011.

Forest treatment: Restore to what? Part 2

The Taos News – Natural Resources Notebook. Jan 27 – Feb 2, 2011. p. B16

A lot of our forest area is too thick and is over-loaded with dead (dry) fuel. Should we be concerned about this? Maybe only where our homes are at risk to loss from fire in the wild land urban interface (WUI)?

The Healthy Forests Restoration Act (H.R.1904-2 of Jan 7, 2003) provides a platform for funding forest treatment. In practice restoration is about going from unhealthy forest conditions to a healthier state, which in turn is a safer state for people and their structures. What is considered an unhealthy forest? It depends on the perspective. From the viewpoint of people living in the WUI it's one that is too thick and has too much dead fuel. It is also one that is too extensive (continuous) without breaks (open spaces). Too thick and continuous means low biological diversity and little spatial (habitat) diversity.

From the perspective of elk, an unhealthy forest is much the same: too thick for grass to grow, not enough open spaces. Too continuous means having to go farther to find food. At the other extreme too large an open area, like from a big fire, also means not having enough cover to hide from predators.

In sort of the "who came first the chicken or the egg?" situation, we can think about where to start in pondering what to restore to. We can start with an unhealthy forest that is as thick as it can get. When it burns, often at high intensity due to the amount of fuel, what follows is a grassland type of vegetation or brush such as Gambel Oak, depending on elevation and aspect (which way the slope faces). This early stage is gradually replaced by tree communities. The rate of replacement depends on habitat. The better the habitat the faster the pace of change. Better usually has to do with moisture. The natural process, in which one plant community is replaced by another after an event like fire, is referred to as ecological succession.

Society must decide which is better: to let Nature take its course (which it will if we preserve without treatment) or to take actions towards healthier forest conditions. It would seem obvious that we are beyond the point of letting nature do it all, considering our desire to live in the WUI or in the forest itself. If we all moved into towns and cities, that might be an option. The best option is to have a balance between natural preserved areas where we don't intervene and treated forest areas. In the latter foresters help Nature along in achieving healthy conditions for the forest and its natural inhabitants. Room to grow (not too thick) and diversity are the key factors in a healthy forest. Habitat diversity leads to biological diversity. Here habitat refers to the living element: open spaces of varying size that provide food for a range of animals: grass for elk, brush for deer and seeds and berries for bear.

Going from an unhealthy state to a healthy one through thinning and timber harvesting is expensive. The key to doing it over significant areas is having a forest industry that can pay for it. Trees removed in thinning should have a value in the market. At the same time this means sustainable jobs and revenue.

But, how do we establish a forest industry?

Forest treatment: Restore to what? Part 3

The Taos News – Natural Resources Notebook. Feb 10 – 16, 2011. p. B6

Forest treatment, as in restoration involving thinning, is expensive. Getting from "too thick" to "just right" involves cutting and removing or treating large numbers of trees. This in turn means lots of wood that can be (and is) used for energy, and potentially a wide range of wood and more high tech energy products.

Who pays for restoration treatment? Without viable forest industry, we all do through taxes. Ideally forest products could pay for treatment. When it's a net cost to taxpayers, it is either limited to fairly small areas or is an excessive burden on the tax-paying public. But how can we have value-added products if we don't have much of a forest industry?

Right now through Collaborative Forest Restoration Program (CFRP) a relatively small amount of forest area is effectively being treated on Forest Service, BLM and private lands. This is in the framework of the Community Wildfire Protection Program (CWPP) and the Firewise program on the wildland-urban interface (WUI) to protect human structures.

Since treatment does not pay its own way it depends on taxpayers' money that is distributed in the form of grants. New Mexico has a very active program with a number of grants distributed every year for on-the-ground treatment and for technological development including monitoring. This plays an important role. But is it sustainable in times of high fiscal deficit and pressures to cut spending?

The question is: How could we expand the area treated without it becoming a politically unsustainable burden on taxpayers? To really make a significant difference, forest treatment costs must get to a place where they can pay their own way. This means having a viable forest industry that pays for wood and timber that is removed in treatment.

Any treatment of a forest stand must be based on the stand itself. The right combination of small and large trees to be removed must be determined. In some cases mostly smaller trees will be removed. In others mostly larger trees. The greater the proportion of large trees, the more likely treatment can pay for itself.

But, how do we establish a forest industry? First of all, there has to be a continuous supply of timber as well as the right economic, legal and taxation conditions. And we need to be willing to accept the fact that forest ecosystems are living resilient entities that can provide timber on a sustainable basis. I refer to this as sustainable productive forest management (SPFM). The economics are not easy, but combining actual wood value with valued environmental services could make it possible.

A modern forest industry that combines energy with value-added wood products should be able to compete in today's outsourced economic world and provide sustainable jobs. The key is to tie elements together to make it competitive. A major potential source of retribution would be from payment for Carbon. The idea is that treated forests grow faster and more net growth means more Carbon removed from the atmosphere.

Sustainable productive forest management (SPFM) and sustainable non-extractive forest management (SNEFM) should be in balance. In any case SPFM is limited to less steep (topography) more accessible forest areas. It is not feasible on most of our Carson Forest, especially in the Sangre de Cristo Mountains.

Are we up to the task of making this possible? Could this be a forestry "Sputnik moment"?

Forest treatment: Restore to what? Part 4

The Taos News – Natural Resources Notebook. Feb 24 – Mar. 2, 2011. p. B12

Forest restoration would seem to imply that it's just about restoring and then nothing else. Are we forgetting that forests grow? That new trees are constantly being born (regeneration)? That most of them die and the survivors grow? When a gap is formed because a tree or group of trees die, it's filled in at first with herbs, grasses and shrubs and then finally with trees. So most of the trees are growing, some faster some slower. As trees grow the forest becomes thicker. So any "restoration" that we do will eventually be undone by Nature and then we'll have to go back and re-restore. And then after that we'll have to go back again and re-re-restore and so on.

The program that we have referred to in this series is CFRP: Collaborative Forest Restoration Program. So could we refer to this continuous never-ending process as involving CFRRRP? Or maybe the "C" should be changed to stand for "Continuous" resulting in a term that better reflects on the process: Continuous Forest Restoration Program.

Is it reasonable to spend resources on restoring (thinning) when the forest just responds by getting thick again? One could say OK it's like cleaning a house. Just because it gets dirty again doesn't mean that we shouldn't clean it. But there is a big difference. The "dirt" (wood) that we "clean" in thinning the forest has, or can have, value for energy and wood products, which in turn should pay for the cleaning. And furthermore it would create jobs. If dirt were gold we wouldn't have to pay anybody to clean our house. We could just make a deal for the cleaners to be able to use the gold.

Before going on we should remember that thinning is the removal of mostly smaller trees. Timber harvesting (logging) is the removal of larger commercial value trees. Going from too thick to just right, thinning out the forest, involves both. In forestry speak just right (not too thick, not too sparse: like Goldilocks) is normal stocking. Stocking is the term for the "thickness" of the forest.

So, restoration is not a one-shot deal. Resilient forest ecosystems respond by growing. We get from too thick to just right; then the forest grows back towards too thick (over-stocked). Growth is a continuous process as long as there is room to grow. Growth is healthy. Growth uses Carbon from the atmosphere, fixing it into woody tissue. (hence the batteries included www.cmb-lwv.com.ve/batteries_included.htm) Energy in chemical form is stored in woody tissue). This the same as energy stored in what used to be woody, plant and animal (dinosaur) tissues for millions of years that we know as fossil fuels: oil, natural gas and coal as well as tars, bituminous sands, etc.

Then why not get back to the basics that have been worked out in forestry for centuries. You harvest to get to normal stocking. Then you periodically harvest timber to remove the growth, leaving the growing stock and soil intact. This essentially is sustainable productive forest management (SPFM). "Sustainable" not only means environmentally sustainable but also economically so. It pays its own way and therefore doesn't depend on grants that may become scarce in tough economic times. This translates into political sustainability.

For this to be possible we need to have a viable forestry industry.

A viable forest industry depends on the products that can be removed in forest treatment. Cost-effective treatment is closely related to the size distribution and quality of timber removed. Large and old trees are important both for wildlife habitat and to generate income and revenue. Somehow a balance must be attained.

LARGE AND OLD TREES: HOW ARE THEY CONNECTED TO FOREST TREATMENT ECONOMIC AND POLITICAL SUSTAINABILITY?

The economics and politics of extensive forest treatment are hampered by putting a size cap on the trees that are to be removed. As a result we may possibly lose more habitat to fire, insect and disease than if we were to allow extraction (harvesting) of designated large and old trees based on pre-treatment forest stand sampling.

Large, old trees and forest health

Old Trees and Forest Health. *The Taos News – Natural Resources Notebook. June 9 - 15, 2011. p. B7*

How can we best protect wildlife, such as the Mexican Spotted Owl, in our forests? Does a complete ban on removal of large trees really guarantee their habitat?

Establishing a maximum size of trees to be removed in forest restoration for better health would appear to be a good thing. Large and old trees are an essential part of wildlife habitat and contribute to over all diversity. However, that doesn't mean that all such trees must be kept in forest ecosystems. Too many of them may not be good taking into account the cost of forest restoration treatment on relatively large areas. Large trees are more valuable for timber than smaller and younger ones and therefore enhance income that can help pay for forest treatment. Making it possible for thinning and fuel reduction to pay for itself will enable us to treat larger areas meaning that we will have larger areas of healthy forest and as a result more and better habitat for wildlife of all sorts.

When we try to preserve too much we run the risk of actually losing more habitat to intense wildfire. The idea of restoration is to try to get back to a more natural fire regime in which catastrophic high intensity wildfire is less likely to happen. The greater risk of losing habitat is related to having forests that are too thick and that have too much fuel. Too thick is not healthy because it means that there is not enough room to grow and growth is healthy. Trees that are growing are physiologically in better shape to withstand fire, insect and disease.

Simplistic measures that don't consider the real conditions of forest ecosystems tend to have unwanted outcomes. Forest ecosystems are very complex things. Their internal dynamics involve many interactions among trees, other plants, animals and the physical habitat. Dealing with them, whether to preserve them or to restore or change them, cannot be approached with simplistic measures such as putting a cap on the size of trees to be removed.

Removing the size cap could actually result in better preservation of endangered species. How could that be?

Consider the connection between preserving an endangered species and imposing a broad encompassing measure that has nothing to do with individual forest stands and ecosystems and their diversity. Thinning a too-thick forest and reducing the fuel load on large areas is costly. Either taxpayers must subsidize such treatment or the treatment can pay for itself. But with a size cap it is more difficult to cover the costs due to the lower value of material removed.

In treatment towards better forest health, large and old trees can be designated to remain. Wildlife biologists can tell the forest managers how many of each kind of tree need to remain in the stands. This means enough for wildlife needs, but not every single one.

Consider two ways to ensure that there are enough large and old trees to enhance wildlife habitat: treat larger areas of forest for forest health without the need for subsidies and have a balance between un-treated areas and those treated for forest health.

I wish to thank our readers for their interest and support. I also think that they will understand my need for a couple of month's vacation. I look forward to continuing this column in the fall.

The preceding article is the last published in the 2007 – Spring 2011 series allowing for a break and concentration on publishing the articles in this book to make the material more readily available. Additional Fall 2011 and winter 2012 articles have been included at the last manuscript revision.

Obviously the articles here are not in chronological order but rather organized by topics. Se from here we go on to some thoughts on forest health. The following is a nine-part series on the idea of establishing a healthy forest buffer zone around critical areas that we want to protect. It is part of the over all idea of achieving a balance between protection and production in forest management.

HEALTHY FOREST BUFFER ZONE (HFBZ) INITIATIVE

The following is a fairly extensive exposition of ideas for a healthy forest initiative building on our discussion of forest management and restoration treatment. The buffer zone was viewed as a strategy of approach that would be acceptable in current environmental thinking. The idea behind all of this is that a balance between SPFM and SNEFM is essential for aver all sustainability in dealing with public and private forests.

We start this lap of our adventure trying to answer the question: What is a healthy forest?

What are the criteria for a healthy forest?

The Taos News – Natural Resources Notebook. March 5 -11, 2009. p. B11

A healthy forest is more resistant to fire, disease and insect damage than an unhealthy one. Obvious. But just what is a healthy forest?

One criterion is related to growth. A forest that is growing vigorously would naturally tend to be healthier than one that is not growing. Since a forest is made up of trees (and lots of other living things) its health is related to the sum of trees' individual health. If most of the trees in the forest are growing vigorously, then the forest as a whole will be growing and therefore, according to the growth criterion, would be a healthy forest. In contrast, if most of the trees were not growing, or just barely growing, the forest as a whole would not be healthy.

A second criterion is related to the degree of diversity in terms of life forms and species (biological diversity or biodiversity), vertical structure (meaning a range of tree sizes) and spatial distribution (meaning the presence of clearings, small open spaces instead of continuous forest canopy). A more diverse forest is healthier than a less diverse one. The implication in management is to have diversity in the forest stand itself regarding tree size distribution and presence of open spaces, in which other species, such as grasses, herbs and bushes can grow, which are also are an important source of food for wildlife.

Another criterion is related to the amount of fuel in the form of standing dead tree-trunks and deadwood on the forest floor. In our climate wood decomposes very slowly. This results in a build-up of fuel and is one of the reasons to have prescribed burning. Low fuel build-up would be an indicator of forest health.

Under what conditions would trees be more likely to grow vigorously? First of all we have to think about what "vigorously" means. In the tropics, vigorous growth is as much as, or more than, an inch in diameter per year and over six feet in height per year, at least when they are young. Obviously, aquí en Taos, "vigorous" growth will be much less. Furthermore, here and in the tropics or anywhere, growth rates vary with species, which means some trees, like aspen, inherently grow faster than others, such as spruce or fir, under the same conditions.

"Under the same conditions" refers to the two other main factors that affect growth: habitat and stand density (the thickness of the forest). In a given climatic area, like North Central New Mexico, habitat involves altitude, aspect and soil. Aspect in forestry means the direction in which the slope is facing. A south-facing slope will be warmer and drier than a north-facing slope. Soil is a major factor, which in turn stems from geology, climate and time. The combination of aspect and soil largely determines what foresters call "site quality", which is an expression of productive capacity (basically growth) and as such will largely determine carrying capacity (the limit of living matter –biomass- that a site can support).

In general growth rates can be studied and quantified under different habitat conditions and under different conditions of forest stand density. As a result vigorous growth and almost stagnant non-growth can be defined for any combination of species and habitat. The objective in sivicultural management focused on forest health would be to make sure that there is room to grow. This means keeping the forest from being too thick. "Too thick" means that the stocking level is too close to carrying capacity. Theoretically, at carrying capacity there is no room to grow, meaning there is no net growth. Net growth is growth beyond what is needed to replace trees that die or are destroyed by wind or other agents. On their own, left to nature, forests gradually become thicker and thicker through growth of individual trees and the process of adding new, addition trees (new trees being born referred to as regeneration). This is countered by mortality just like in any living population. The thicker the forest is, the greater the competition there is among trees for sunlight, moisture and soil nutrients.

Summarizing, conditions for a healthy forest involve growth, diversity and low fuel build-up. All three of these can be manipulated or modified through management and in doing so, like through thinning, forest products can be obtained, including energy while at the same time providing jobs. Are we willing to consider doing this?

This article was a first look at the matter of forest health published in March, 2009. It led to the following nine-part series in which the idea and proposal is pursued in further depth.

Healthy forests, management and jobs: Part 1 (of the 9-article series)

The Taos News – Natural Resources Notebook. Dec 17 – 23, 2009. p. B8

Many of our public forests are over-stocked; they're too thick meaning that they are unhealthy. This has two major implications: first, it means that much of our forest area is at a greater than needed risk to loss from fire, insect and disease (or any combination of them); second, it means we are losing growth potential, which in turn means that we are missing an opportunity to take more CO_2 out of the atmosphere through photosynthesis and that we are "wasting" site productivity that could provide wood products, energy and jobs.

Creating healthy forest buffer zones around wilderness areas, critical high-country watersheds and other priority areas could help protect them from fire while at the same time providing other benefits, especially jobs. This could be an effective economic and renewable energy permanent stimulus that would be economically as well as environmentally sustainable. The idea is that a healthy growing, not-too-thick forest with reduced deadwood fuel accumulation, is more resistant to fire, insect and disease than an unhealthy forest, while tree removal and wood processing involved in the process would have great potential for creating permanent jobs in our northern New Mexico, upper Rio Grande area.

A case in point: the Hondo Fire in 1996, that went from our small community to the top of Flag Mountain above La Lama and Questa, destroying a number of homes in La Lama, in a matter of hours, might have been stopped had there been a healthy forest buffer zone extending from the edge of the San Cristobal valley to the base of the mountains. We will never know, of course, but fire fighters would have had a better chance if the pinyon-juniper forest interspersed with ponderosa pine in the canyons had been thinned and deadwood fuel reduced through prescribed burning. A condition related to, and necessary for, thinning and effective safe prescribed burning is a balanced, moderate road density in the area. Achieving healthy forest conditions in the wild land urban interface (WUI) and in a wider comprehensive buffer zone could eventually significantly reduce loss to catastrophic fires.

The process of getting to a healthy forest place from an unhealthy one involves reducing the stocking level (the "thickness") and the amount of deadwood (dry fuel). "Reducing the stocking level" means making the forest less thick through timber harvesting and thinning. Theoretically there is a point where stocking is so high that there is no net growth. This is the carrying capacity or site potential. All the resources (water, soil nutrients and others) are "used up". Growth only takes place to replace mortality. This can be considered an unhealthy condition.

Ideal, or at least "good enough", stocking can be maintained through successive treatments. A good stocking interval can be defined in terms of basal area and stand density (trees/acre) in which growth is the maximum possible given the combination of forest species and habitat, mainly soil (foresters refer to it as site quality). Theoretically there is a minimum stocking level below which growth in terms of biomass per acre diminishes, basically meaning that there is wasted space (too much room to grow). There is also a stocking level above which growth declines due to over-crowding: not enough room to grow. The optimum is the "just enough room to grow but none wasted". This essentially is the concept of "normal stocking".

The knowledge and technology exist to make a part of our forests healthier and offer a fascinating area of study for our students interested in forestry, natural resources and environmental sciences.

Creating a healthy forest buffer zone: Part 2 (room to grow and diversity)

The Taos News – Natural Resources Notebook. Jan 14 – 20, 2010. p. B7

The major criterion is that there be room to grow; that the forest is not too thick. The level of stocking, the degree to which the forest stand occupies the site and uses resources, is a major factor. Another factor is biological diversity. A healthy forest should have the highest level of biological diversity that the habitat (combination of climate, microclimate and soil) can allow. We can think in terms of microhabitat diversity. An example would be clearings, open spaces in the forest that allow plant species that normally wouldn't be found under the forest canopy.

How the forest stand is made up of different sizes of trees of a given species or group of species is another form of diversity. We can refer to it as structural diversity, which can be expressed in terms of the variation in size (height and diameter) of individual trees or clumps of same-size trees. The degree of "clumpiness" is related in part to shade tolerance. Intolerants tend to form even-aged stands that can be relatively small "clumps" or fairly extensive more or less uniform stands. Shade tolerants on the other hand tend to be more "individualistic" meaning that size variation is on the scale of individual trees. (www.cmb-lwv.com.ve/ shade_tolerance.htm NRN June 25 – July 1, 2009)

Spatial diversity has to do with open spaces created by various events that are very much a part of forest ecosystem dynamics. In forest treatment we can provide for them. They enhance biological diversity.

Dry fuel accumulation is an additional criterion. Too much dry woody matter (fallen trees, branches), leaves and pine needles increase the intensity of fire. So in our healthy forest buffer zone (HFBZ) we should avoid excessive fuel buildup usually through prescribed burning. In certain critical areas such as along roads and around buildings, pruning lower branches helps keep fire from getting into the forest canopy.

As we can see, diversity in all its forms and expressions is good for forest health. A more diverse forest ecosystem is more resilient than a less diverse one. Resiliency is the capacity of an ecosystem to recuperate from alterations. We can think of it as a sort of natural healing process. Nature has provided forest ecosystems with plants and often combinations of plants and animals that close wounds much like callous and scar tissue in our bodies. Often these are "gap fillers". They heal gaps caused by individual trees or groups of trees that are blown down, killed by insects or disease or simply die of old age. The gaps help to enhance habitat diversity by providing open spaces that are then covered by the "healers", which often provide food for wildlife.

Forest health: room to grow, biological, structural and spatial diversity and low dry fuel accumulation on the ground. A good balance between productive healthy forest management and non-treatment management for preservation is a logical sustainable strategy. How do we do it?

Creating a healthy forest buffer zone: Part 3 (more on room to grow)

The Taos News – Natural Resources Notebook. Jan 28 – Feb 03, 2010. pp. B10, B11

The idea of creating and maintaining healthy forest buffer zones around wilderness areas, critical high-country watersheds and other priority areas to help protect them involves developing a sustainable forest management strategy focused on forest health. In a nutshell, forest health is having room to grow, biological, structural and spatial diversity and low dry fuel accumulation on the ground and healthy soil (another matter). We will go into ideas on how to achieve a good balance between sustainable productive healthy forest management and non-treatment management for preservation in a logical sustainable strategy.

We'll continue on the "how to do it" part, starting with making and keeping adequate room to grow. This is a challenge in that it requires long-term thinking and some fairly complex concepts that are not new to forestry and forest management in particular. However, they seem to have fallen out of the picture on our public forests over public concern of sustainability.

One area of thinking involves the use of math and computer forest stand models that help to understand the dynamics of growth, regeneration (new tree establishment) and mortality. Here's a fascinating area of interdisciplinary endeavor for our faculty and students to make contributions while teach in the learning process.

One way to look at it is using a generalized population growth logistic function or "S-shaped" (sigmoid) curve. The math and statistics are complicated but not impossible for the inquisitive young mind, thus the challenge. Stated briefly and simplified, we can identify certain parameters or elements that don't directly involve the math. The two most direct elements (they can be referred to as variables in the model) are: 1) zero biomass, which would be the starting point for the population curve and in our forest ecosystem model could be, for example, the point at which we are after an intensive fire (consider the Hondo Burn where it jumped the old highway north of San Cristobal) in which biomass, as expressed in terms of basal area (BA), is zero; 2) carrying capacity where biomass is the maximum that the site can support. The latter is where the S-curve levels off. What happens in between these two points is the difficult part. Regeneration, growth and mortality take place in ecological succession in which different plant communities replace each other. Biomass (simplified in terms of BA) increases slowly at first, gradually picking up speed until a theoretical point of inflection occurs as competition begins to affect growth rates. From that point on, the rate of growth gradually declines approaching carrying capacity. The real curve (basal area related to time) with its point of inflection will not be a smooth one, but rather bumpy. Models constitute a simplification of reality. How well they represent it can be determined through statistical analyses.

For more on carrying capacity and basal area, see www.cmb-lwv.com.ve/carrying_capacity.htm (Most of the Natural Resources Notebook articles can be found at www.cmb-lwv.com.ve/guide_ttn_nrn.htm).

We'll introduce two forest stocking (the "how thick" matter) variables as guidelines in our model. The first is an experimentally determined level of stocking (too thick) above which growth is slower than desired (within the limits of the tree species and habitat, mainly soil and climate). The second is the level below which growth is too little because the site is not fully occupied (too "thin"). More on stocking control in Part 4.

Getting to "just right" in stand stocking involves some highly technical elements, which are pretty much beyond the scope of our thinking here. Our readers will find some repetition, keeping in mind that this is a series of articles in which great effort has been made to explain matters in terms that are accessible to the general public. For the more adventurous, exploring concepts, such as normal stocking will be challenging but well worth the effort. Going into forest stand growth models and a systems approach in general, will further enhance our adventure.

Creating a healthy forest buffer zone: Room to grow and jobs Part 4

The Taos News – Natural Resources Notebook. Feb 11 - 17, 2010. p. B6

Right now, on the political front, there is a lot of talk of stimulus money and what it's achieving. The bottom line: jobs.

Providing room to grow, in getting to a healthy forest state, is part of the idea of creating and maintaining healthy forest buffer zones around wilderness areas, critical high-country watersheds and other priority areas to help protect them. Getting to a healthy forest state and then keeping it there has great potential to create permanent, sustainable jobs, both in the woods in the preparation of areas, treatment and post treatment (involving follow-up monitoring) and in forest industry, which unfortunately is very limited at present.

In review, forest health is having room to grow, biological, structural and spatial diversity and low dry fuel accumulation on the ground and healthy soil. Here, we'll continue on the "how to do it" part, concerning making and keeping adequate room to grow and the use of models.

The population growth logistic function or "S-shaped" curve, that expresses biomass growth (using basal area as an approximation) as a function of time, can be separated into two parts: the geometric progression in which growth starts slowly and then increases at an ever increasing rate; the second part, which represents going from the fastest growth that the combination of site (habitat) and forest community (the total number of trees species) can get and slowly decreases as total biomass approaches carrying capacity. The place where the curve changes trend is the point of inflection. The only sure places on the curve are the starting point (like after a fire: biomass is zero) and the level where net growth ceases at the carrying capacity. The rest of the curve, what happens between them) is challenging. The treatment model involves two forest stocking level points in our model: the "too thick" level of basal area (above which growth is slower than desired) and the "too sparse" level below which growth is too slow because the stand is under-stocked. The idea is first to get close to the too sparse level and then to maintain stocking between the two levels. Thinning takes place when stocking gets near the too thick level.

Any model that tries to describe this dynamic process is a simplification of reality. An interesting area for our mathematically inclined students would be to study the model, starting out by doing library and Internet research into the matter. The raw data to develop and test such a model comes from samples taken in stands of different ages, through the use of permanent plots that can be measured repeatedly over time or the intrinsic growth record that trees keep in the form of annual rings (through a process called stem analysis). There are specialized stand stocking models such as the Reineke's Stand Density Index. We don't have to re-invent the wheel on this but learn to use the tools available that have been developed over the course of at least two centuries in Europe and the US.

Most of the Natural Resources Notebook articles can be found at www. cmb-lwv.com.ve/guide_ttn_nrn.htm

We still have to consider how to pay for treatment. The key is a strategy involving establishing forest industry adapted to the forest potential. More on this in Part 5.

Creating a healthy forest buffer zone key to sustainability: Part 5

The Taos News – Natural Resources Notebook. Feb 25 – March 3, 2010. p. B9

A key element in the economic aspect of sustainability (which translates into political sustainability) in creating and maintaining a healthy forest buffer zone (HFBZ) is getting a forest industry established, which needs to be adapted to the forest stands in the buffer zone; adapted both in terms of sizes of trees to use and the rate of harvesting, which, once the room-to-grow state is achieved, must not exceed net growth.

Before we go on into more details of how to create a healthy forest as part of a strategy to protect preserved areas from wildfire, we'll suggest an example with assumed information that should help to understand the idea. We'll assume a total initial (pilot demo projects) area of 50,000 acres of HFBZ out of a total of more than 1.5 million acres total forest area in our Carson National Forest. This would amount to less than 3% since the HFBZ would include some areas of other public lands and also private lands. The 50,000-acre buffer zone would not be in one continuous area but distributed according to topography, accessibility and forest conditions. It would include different types of forest ranging from pinyon-juniper (P-J) to ponderosa and some spruce-fir and aspen at higher elevations that are part of the wild land urban interface (WUI) along roads and around population centers (towns and villages such as Red River and Taos Ski Valley).

There are two stages in the process: first, getting to the right room-to-grow stocking level; then maintaining the healthy room-to-grow forest state through repeated thinning and timber harvesting treatments. This is done on a forestry-related time scale. Foresters are accustomed to dealing with longer timeframes than most activities. So "repeated" thinning would involve treatments at intervals of, for example, 50 years or more. For example, the buffer zone forest would be thinned every 50 years (this is the cutting cycle). The actual interval between thinning depends on the forest ecosystem's response in terms of growth, which is determined through continuous monitoring, in which the public would be involved.

Going from too thick to just right will produce a certain amount of woody biomass. We'll assume that going, for example, from a basal area of 100 to 60 sq.ft. / acre will produce 400 cubic feet of wood per acre in one treatment. This will depend on the actual characteristics of the forest stands; first of all regarding what type of forest we're dealing with in each case. A P-J forest stand will have a smaller yield than a stand with a fairly good proportion of ponderosa pine. Stand variables will need to be estimated prior to treatment. Keeping basal area between 60 and 80 sq.ft./acre would involve periodic harvesting of the amount of wood that results from growth during the cycle.

Treatment of fairly extensive areas in the HFBZ will not be feasible without income generated from the process. The main source of income would be from forest products, which means getting an adequately adapted forest industry established to create value-added products while at the same time creating permanent, sustainable jobs, generating revenue, providing a source of renewable energy and, hopefully, getting paid for carbon sequestering (a growing forest takes more CO_2 out of the atmosphere).

Diversity a factor in creating a healthy forest buffer: Part 6

The Taos News – Natural Resources Notebook. March 11-17, 2010. p. B5

Looking around us we can see areas that seem to be all the same, meaning the appearance of little diversity. An example would be our sagebrush. A similar observation would be our pinyon-juniper (P-J) forests that from a distance appear to be the same all over except when we compare south facing to north facing slopes (aspects). If we look closely we will see more diversity, but much less than if we look at areas along one of our streams. Diversity is important.

In addition to having room to grow, diversity is a major factor in forest ecosystem health. Generally the more diverse an ecosystem the healthier it is, largely due to its greater stability and resilience in recovering from natural or human alterations.

There are different types of diversity. The most common is biological diversity or biodiversity, which involves the number of species and genetic variation within species in an ecosystem. Another is spatial or horizontal diversity, which involves open spaces and clumps of varying density. Structural (vertical) diversity is another form of diversity, which has to do with different ages and sizes of trees. Different forest stands have inherent tendencies in size diversity. A shade-tolerant forest species tends to naturally have greater structural diversity than an intolerant species. This is a result of the regeneration and growth characteristics. A shade tolerant species regenerates and grows under its own shade or the shade of other species (see www.cmb-lwv.com.ve/shade_tolerance.htm).

Regarding structural diversity, foresters use what is called a stand table, which describes a forest stand in terms of the number of trees and basal area by size categories, usually using diameter at breast height (DBH; diameter classes). This gives a sort of a vertical cross-section of the stand. We have stands where most of the trees are fairly large, with few smaller trees. This would be typical of a shade intolerant species such as aspen. In contrast, a common situation for a shade tolerant species (spruces and firs) would be to have a decreasing number of trees as size increases (more trees in smaller DBH classes than in large ones). This is a result of a continuous regeneration process in which new trees are being born constantly with a few surviving and growing into larger diameter classes, due to their ability to tolerate shade.

Biodiversity can be enhanced in creating a healthy forest by making open spaces of varying sizes, which create the conditions for tree and other plant species that are not typically present in abundance in continuous canopy forest stands, largely due to shading. These open spaces allow herbs, grasses and shrubs to grow, which are a source of food for animals thus enhancing animal diversity.

Structural diversity can be achieved through treatment by selectively removing trees according to size. We would start with stand table information from sampling and thus prescribe treatment in terms of removal by DBH classes. This means that treatment, thinning and timber harvesting, will be free from pre-established restrictions. The treatment is prescribed directly from the diagnosis.

The end result of creating open spaces and selective removal of trees according to size will improve forest health in our proposed buffer zone to enhance the protection of critical wilderness and watershed areas.

Reduced dry biomass part of healthy forest buffer zone: Part 7

The Taos News – Natural Resources Notebook. March 25-31, 2010. p. B6

A forest with too much dry fuel is not healthy. In our climate dry matter takes a longtime to decay. Decay is nature's recycling process of taking care of biomass and what it's made of: mostly carbon. The carbon in dead tissues (and of course living also) comes from the atmosphere in the form of CO2, the same stuff we're trying to reduce. Think of the carbon cycle. The Carbon in CO2 goes from the atmosphere into plant tissues (photosynthesis) where it's turned into carbohydrates, which are a source of food (energy) used in tissue building as part of the physiological processes in trees and other plants.

Obviously, the more dry fuel there is in the form of dead trees and branches, the greater the risk of a fire spreading out of control. In the last articles we have been dealing with removal of live trees in thinning and timber harvesting in creating a healthy forest buffer zone, having room to grow and different types of diversity, namely biological, spatial and structural.

A forest ecosystem develops fairly large amounts of dry biomass as the result of mortality of individual trees or clumps of trees due to natural causes related to longevity or related to events such as bark beetles and wind. Another source of dry, dead biomass is through the dying of lower branches as the tree grows in height, as a result of competition. Theoretically lower branches are less efficient at producing "food" (photosynthesis) because they are less exposed to sunlight; that they get to a point where they consume more than they produce and cease to be an advantage for the tree's health. As a result such branches die providing fuel ladders for fire to get into the crowns.

How can we reduce or manage dry fuel? One way that has been a tool for humans since prehistoric times, is fire. Prescribed burning is an economical tool for fuel reduction. It also can accelerate nutrient cycling in the soil and provides valuable fire control training although, unfortunately, sometimes can result in wildfire. We remember the fire at Los Alamos.

A more expensive alternative is physical (mechanical) treatment or removal of dead fuel. One way is wood gathering. However this only removes the thicker material. Fine material consisting of twigs, leaves and pine needles will remain. It would not be practical to rake and gather such material on large areas. We can do this around our houses and along our fences to protect them. Chipping is an alternative and can be an attractive one in that chips are more quickly integrated into the soil that other material. Again, chipping is expensive unless the resulting material can be used in some way that helps pay for treatment. One possibility is for energy. Research and development are needed to further explore wood chips as a viable source of energy either in solid (possibly to generate electricity) or liquid form (wood ethanol). This is actually another form of solar energy (see www.cmb-lwv.com.ve/living_solar_panels.htm) in which the living forest leaf biomass acts as a huge complex solar panel.

Finding a way to pay for treatment is a challenge in creating a healthy forest buffer zone that involves getting added value forest products and compensation for environmental services (carbon sequestering and oxygen).

Healthy soil is part of healthy forest buffer zone Part 8

The Taos News – Natural Resources Notebook. April 8 - 14, 2010

Maintaining a healthy soil is an important part of forest health in creating a healthy forest buffer zone (HFBZ) to protect our forest watersheds and wilderness areas, in addition to having room to grow; biological, spatial and structural diversity; and low levels of dead biomass.

Keeping a forest soil healthy in forest ecosystems is a key to enhancing resiliency, which is the intrinsic ability of a forest ecosystem to recuperate from natural or human alterations such as fire. Nature has built in the capacity of ecosystems to survive even the most intensive, apparently destructive, events provided that the soil is not irreversibly damaged. And, considering longer, geologic time scales, given a set of climatic conditions and a leftover substrate (even bare rock), the ecosystem will come back, starting with the soil-building process. It's all a question of timescale; how long we (or nature) are willing to wait. Nature has plenty of time.

Wood and timber removal involves the use of machinery and even sometimes animal traction (oxen and mules), which obviously have an impact on the soil. The main impact is compaction and rut formation, mostly in skidding, which is the moving of logs and other woody material from stump to loading site. Modern skidders have been designed to minimize compaction as well as move logs faster. Large tire wheel skidders have much less impact on the soil than the old track bulldozers, which are slower and harder on the soil. Another example of soil impact mitigation is through optimization of the network of skid trails, loading sites and access roads.

Roads obviously are an essential element of timber harvesting (logging) and continued management that involves stand treatment such as slash treatment, prescribed burning, further thinning, possibly stump reduction in recreational areas and a most important element: monitoring of forest ecosystem response over time.

Road network design (layout) and construction techniques can mitigate soil impact, including erosion. Network optimization can minimize the amount of road needed per unit of area, which can be expressed in terms of miles of road per 1000-acre unit. Road layout in accordance with topography is an important factor, as are construction details and post treatment maintenance of selected roads needed for treatment and monitoring. Law enforcement is needed to control access.

The technology to mitigate impact on forest soils exists. The question is mostly regarding the economics of its application in relatively large areas of HFBZ. Paying for it, along with the rest of forest treatment activity, requires that material woody products and environmental services (CO_2 uptake, water and oxygen and aesthetics) have value-added status. An adequate forest industry adapted to the forest potentials in terms of wood species and sizes as well as growth is an important element. Assigning value to Carbon sequestering (fixation in wood that is periodically removed from the ecosystem) and other environmental and human services is another source of economic retribution. "Green" certification based on multi-party monitoring is a needed credibility element in the equation.

It's doable if we decide to take this route in a relatively small portion of our forest resources. Striking a suitable balance between HFBZ managed forest and preserved areas is the answer to full environmental, economic (including jobs) and social (political) sustainability.

Recap: Having a healthy forest buffer zone: Part 9

The Taos News – Natural Resources Notebook. April 22 - 28, 2010. p. B5

This is the last in a series on creating a healthy forest buffer zone that could help to protect critical wilderness areas, high mountain watersheds, forests of spiritual value and other areas that we wish to preserve without human alteration. Furthermore, the idea in general is to strike a sustainable balance between treated and non-treated public forests. In either case forest management is based on sound forest ecology. We manage a protected (preserved) area in that it involves defining objectives, planning and decision-making (especially regarding fire control), trail maintenance and law enforcement, all of which involve human and financial resources. Protecting (preservation) is not a matter of just legislating and leaving it alone.

In most things in life, including politics and ideology, extremes are unsustainable. Trying to over-protect is just as unwise as under-protecting. Setting aside too large a proportion of our forests ends up exposing them to natural events related to extremes in forest density and fuel build-up. Likewise not setting aside enough areas exposes forests to excessive human alteration. An example of a sustainable balance could be a 30 – 70 ratio: a healthy forest buffer zone of 30% of a given forest leaving 70% unaltered.

The strategy would involve designating pilot projects within the buffer zone to explore the productive potential, work out economic issues and establish demonstration areas for the public through a progressive, stage-wise approach, starting with relatively small areas. A key component of the idea regarding economic sustainability is creating a forest industry that is adapted to the needs and productive potential of the buffer zone forests. Forest treatment is expensive, especially on the scale under consideration here. The idea is to establish pilot areas to gain public support and to work out the economics.

The idea to start with is to set up a project formulation and evaluation stage that would lead to a viable step-wise project starting with pilot scale forest treatment areas and forest industry. Partnerships would be established with governmental, educational, private business and non-governmental entities to formulate and evaluate this healthy forest buffer zone proposal that would lead to a viable project that can be "sold" to deciding entities, meaning legislative and executive braches of federal, state and local governments and businesses. Such a project would need to be evaluated from the R & D perspective, meaning that it would require funding during the pilot stage. The idea is for it to be environmentally, economically and politically sustainable.

- Protection: Healthy forest surrounds critical areas.

- Forest treatment: Getting to and maintaining a healthy forest involves thinning and timber harvesting providing wood products and energy.

- Economic sustainability: Forest industries adapted to the buffer zone forests.

- Jobs: Forest treatment and industry provide jobs and revenue.

- Climate change mitigation: Healthy forests take up more carbon (CO_2) through enhanced growth (biomass removal) than untreated forests.

- Renewable energy: Forest biomass energy obtained from treatment is a reality (our firewood, wood pellets) and a huge potential source of energy (electricity from woodchips, liquid bio-fuel).

- Environmental and political sustainability: "Green" certification and public monitoring improve credibility.

Let's consider the advantages of establishing a balance between productively managed healthy forests and preserved untreated forest areas whether in a buffer zone or under a different strategy. The key to true environmental, economic and socio-political sustainability is balance.

A final take on the idea of a healthy forest buffer zone to help protect a sensitive area, such as a relatively small wilderness area in the Carson National Forest of Northern New Mexico. This could be taken as a practical example of the HFBZ idea. The following is the last article submitted to the Taos News in 2011.

Wilderness and healthy forest buffer zone: The Columbine-Hondo area

Columbine-Hondo a healthy forest buffer zone. *The Taos News – Natural Resources Notebook. Jan 5 – 11, 2012. p. B8, B9*

Over all environmental, economic and socio-political sustainability of forests and other wild lands demands a balance between preservation and productive management. Preserved wilderness areas are essential. An approach to balance would be to have healthy forest buffer zones surrounding protected areas in which sustainable productive management practices would be applied.

It appears that the proposed Columbine-Hondo wilderness area has support from a wide range of people and organizations. The area includes a spectacular conglomeration of forests, meadows, tundra and rock outcrops. It includes important watersheds, big and small, like our San Cristobal creek. The high country offers a variety of recreational values and environmental services and is quite naturally a wilderness area with only trails as human improvements.

The idea of the designation of this as a wilderness area is a good one. However, ideally a wilderness area of this sort should be surrounded by a buffer zone of forests treated to reduce fuels and enhance biological and habitat diversity, which would serve to help protect the area from wildfire, while at the same time resulting in healthier forests and much needed jobs. The wildland-urban interface (WUI, pronounced wooie), that's found around communities, like San Cristobal, and around highways, will always be a potential source of wildfire from human activities. Such a buffer zone would make it more likely to be able to stop a fire such as the Hondo fire before it gets into the high country wilderness area.

An additional benefit of such a buffer zone would be to have more people involved in woodcutting, thinning, timber harvesting and forest industry, which provide sustainable jobs. People whose livelihood depends on the forest are more likely to be more active in wildfire prevention. Roads in the buffer zone would facilitate fire suppression as well as treatment.

Healthy forest, as used here, means room to grow (not too thick, not overstocked); optimized biological, spatial (habitat) and structural diversity; reduced dead fuel accumulation; and healthy soils. Structural diversity has to do with tree size distribution (diameter distribution). Provisions can be made regarding sufficient large and old trees for wildlife habitat. This is a part of structural diversity. Forest management technology is available to implement this strategy, much of it involving the use of forest stand growth models to evaluate and predict outcomes in the planning stage. Multi-party follow up monitoring is essential in the continuous evaluation of the forest ecosystems' responses to treatment.

An eventual healthy forest buffer zone would be composed of suitable forest, which would be designated based on topography, soil and forest conditions using geographic information system (GIS) technology.

Another issue is fire suppression. Does managing a wilderness area include fire control? Would natural lightning fires be put out? Would "heavier" fire suppression like air tanker support be allowed? Or, would there be a let-burn policy? Would we accept a large fire in a relatively small wilderness area? It's not a question of "if" but "when" on a long time scale. These questions are not easy to answer but must be addressed.

The proposal here is to create a healthy forest buffer zone surrounding the proposed wilderness area, in which sustainable productive forest management practices would be carried out on a permanent basis. This would create a model for similar areas and contribute greatly to over all environmental, economic and political sustainability of wilderness areas.

There is a lot more to forest health than would be considered at a simple glance. Obviously there also is a lot of controversy on the matter. Regardless of one's point of view, it's imperative that basic ecological concepts be understood. A simplistic view of forest health can be misleading. Enough said on the subject for now. Now for some reflections and somewhat personal comments as the end of 2009 marks just over two years of the Natural Resources Notebook. The last article of the year was dedicated to reflections on global climate change with a brief pitch for the UNM-Taos Forest Ecology course and more thoughts on the potential role of SPFM in climate change mitigation.

Reflections on 2009 and hopes for 2010

The Taos News – Natural Resources Notebook. Dec 31, 2009 – Jan 6, 2010. p. B10

We are ending the old year. 2009 brought us some interesting and challenging matters. Among them, the Copenhagen global climate summit, which although didn't result in firm binding resolutions, put forth commitments that will pave the way for progress. Another matter hopefully shared with the readers of The Taos News Natural Resources Notebook, is the end of another full year of this column. I've had positive feedback, which I sincerely appreciate. I look forward to more interactions in the coming year. I wish to express my appreciation to The Taos News for continued support in the Natural Resource Notebook and to UNM-Taos for support pointing out that all opinions expressed are my own and do not reflect university policy. I would like to invite readers to my Forest Ecology spring semester 2010 course at UNM-T. There are no prerequisites. You can find it on p. 16 of the catalog under Biology (BIOL 299). It's a topic course with lots of discussion on subjects including tropical forestry. Auditing (no tests!) is a stress-less option for students of all ages.

One matter that seems to have been considered in Copenhagen is a different way of thinking on the part of private sector, including major corporations, often seen as culprits. Forestry and specifically forest management has been mentioned, mostly on the sidelines. The role of forest management in climate change mitigation merits our attention. Forests and plant communities in general play a role in taking CO_2 out of the atmosphere through photosynthesis. There are two aspects of the matter: forests as a carbon reserve (carbon in forest biomass); the other has to do with rates of carbon take-up related to growth. A forest that is growing is taking more Carbon out of the atmosphere than one that is at full capacity (carrying capacity) where growth only takes replace to replace biomass lost to mortality. This means that where there is room to grow, more CO_2 is removed from the atmosphere and fixed into woody biomass. This is part of what a healthy forest is: room to grow. What we do with the woody biomass is crucial. It must be removed periodically to maintain room to grow. That which we remove can remain fixed in wood products. That which we turn into energy returns CO2 to the atmosphere in the burning (oxidation) process meaning carbon neutrality.

It should be clear that no matter what our view is on global warming, we should take solidly thought out actions towards reducing CO2 and other greenhouse gas emissions, if for no other reason but the precautionary principle. It makes sense to take actions in any way that will be effective and not hurt our economy. It will take concerted effort on public agencies, such as the Forest Service and BLM, the private sector (and yes, there has to be profit motivation) and non-governmental entities (NGO's), to achieve realistic objectives. Forest management towards getting to healthy forests on a portion of our public and private forests (including our local land grants) offers a real opportunity to mitigate climate change while at the same time generating much needed jobs in our area and a truly green renewable energy source beyond our traditional firewood, which plays an important role in our economy, culture and tradition.

Best wishes for a happy holiday season and a better 2010 for all.

Having considered forest restoration and treatment, the role of large and old trees and the concept of forest health, we're ready to go into the real world of forest industry and its role in society: economics, politics, environment and general sustainability. So, our adventure leads us on to the role of forest industry in making forest treatment possible and in achieving a sustainable balance in our approach to dealing with public and private forests.

THE ROLE OF FOREST INDUSTRY: FOREST HEALTH, INDUSTRY, RENEWABLE ENERGY AND JOBS

Significant treatment for forest health cannot be achieved without a viable, sustainable forest industry. Sustainability must be in economic and political terms as well as environmental. Modern efficient, and, yes, sustainable industry must cover a wide range of products and services, renewable energy probably being the most important. Industry as used here includes both solid and liquid wood-based energy options. Distributed generation of electricity probably offers the greatest immediate potential, though there are many economic and technological challenges. This offers a great opportunity for our young people in developing challenging, meaningful, enjoyable and productive careers.

Forest industry and forest health

The Taos News – Natural Resources Notebook. March 10 – 16, 2011. p. B13

Why would it be desirable to establish a modern forest industry in our area or for that matter in any area where there is a significant amount of forest?

In the previous, last, series of four articles on forest restoration it would seem obvious that in order to be able to treat a significant area of forest there must be a means to make it pay for itself. It should not have to rely on taxpayers' money in the form of grants. The bottom line: economic and political sustainability.

What would a modern forest industry look like? It would depend on the forest conditions, the types of forest available. It would further depend on the objectives both of forest treatment and the industry itself.

Sustainable renewable energy should be at the top of the list. What if we decide to dedicate a relatively small portion of our public and private forests to sustainable productive forest management, that involves treatment that takes the forest to a place where it is healthy and then keeps it there through repeated treatments. This may sound drastic. Let's use some numbers to illustrate. First of all, in forestry we are used to using a combination of large areas and long spans of time (in human terms). For example repeatedly treating the same area of forest depends on growth. In our area where growth is slow, it would be common to use a cutting cycle of, for example, 50 years. This means that we would go back and re-treat the forest every 50 years. The first step is to get to the just right thickness: normal stocking. A place where forests stands are not too thick and not too sparse. "Too thick" means not enough room to grow and "too sparse" means wasted growing space. Then, once there, the main treatment in the form of timber harvesting (logging) would take place when the forest reaches a thickness (stocking) where we start to see growth diminish. At that point stocking is reduced to the minimum level where we still get the best growth. So every 50 years (if growth determines that) we adjust stocking by removing trees. Besides the main treatment (timber harvesting), there would be additional silvicultural treatments to do various things, like maintaining roads (sustainable road network built to specifications that protect soil), thinning over-stocked areas, possible planting in under-stocked areas, pruning and, of course fire control and law enforcement.

"Large areas" mean that we can divide a given designated productive area (as in our example) into 50 one-year areas and each one will be big enough to produce an amount of timber that can sustain a forest industry. This is an over-simplified example, just to help us along with the reasoning. In reality we would not expect a given forest area to sustain a given industry but optimize by combining areas and diversifying the industry. If, for example producing electricity from wood chips were the main objective, we might have several plants distributed so that transportation costs (the main cost in logging) is kept optimally low. And we would integrate production with other wood products.

Having a viable sustainable multi-product and service forest industry is key to having a large area of healthy forest, especially in the WUI. Balance in our public and private forest policy is critical to over all sustainability.

Forest industry: Part 2

The Taos News – Natural Resources Notebook. March 24 – 30, 2011. p. B9

A viable sustainable multi-product and service forest industry is key to having a large area of healthy forest. Industry means a complex network of wood processing plants, a major part of which could for energy.

Feasibility of such an industry depends on an array of factors: timber supply, costs, infrastructure, qualified labor, market conditions and legal regulatory framework; and the willingness on the part of the public to consider it on public forests.

A sustainable flow of timber (wood) depends on having a large enough area of suitable forest. "Large enough" means that long rotations or cutting cycles can be accommodated and still have annual areas big enough to provide a supply of raw material (wood). Example: A 50-year cutting cycle and an assumed 5000-acre annual harvest area resulting in a 250,000-acre net productive management area. This is relatively small in forestry terms. "Suitable" forest means topographic and stand conditions under which timber harvesting can be done economically without damaging the soil. "Stand conditions" mean having enough standing timber to ensure remaining growing stock after removal of timber. Growing stock is like the principal that is left in a savings account to have enough interest (growth) for the future.

A fairly simple statement involving two terms (large enough forest area and suitable forest) leads to a series of forestry and economic terms.

The matter of costs has much to do with distances from timber harvest sites to processing mills. Transportation accounts for a major part of costs of wood at the mill site. It also has to do with topography and road infrastructure. In sustainable productive forest management the stumpage value of timber (standing timber) is gotten by starting with the value of products, discounting processing and consecutively discounting (subtracting) the costs of each of the sequential operations, such as unloading, transportation, loading, skidding (moving logs from the stump to the loading site) and felling.

The human aspect is largely having a trained workforce. Modern equipment, especially skidders, requires skill and experience. Student or youth power in developing innovative technology will be a major factor.

Market conditions are part of the environment of forest industry. The market sets prices that are the framework within which industry does business. However marketing and public policy play an important role, which leads us to considering the legal, regulatory framework. Federal, state and local policies, laws, ordinances and taxes play a major role in feasibility.

An important consideration is public vs. private forests. The owners of public forest, such as the Carson National Forest, are all of us. In the end we will determine what is done or not done, although not directly. We delegate management to public authorities. Our collective opinion has great bearing on forest uses. As a result, and naturally so, management of public forests tends to be more conservative. In contrast, private forest owners can pretty much decide what is to be done. The power of them getting together in various forms of alliances is having large enough areas to make sustainable productive forest management feasible on at least part of their forests.

The key is adapting a forest industry to the forest through specialized products and services and by dealing with large areas to compensate low growth. Balance between sustainable productive forest management and "sustainable non-extractive forest management" in our public and private forest policy is critical to over all sustainability.

Balance in forest policy key to sustainability: Forest industry part 3

The Taos News – Natural Resources Notebook. April 7 – 13, 2011. p. B9

This is a follow up on the idea that in order to be able to treat large areas of forest towards healthy forests, we need to have a viable, economically sustainable multi-product and environmental service forest industry; and on the idea that balance in our forest policy is critical to over all sustainability.

Foresters are used to dealing with large areas and long lengths of time: a half a million acres and 50 to 100 years would be a common situation for management plans. One problem we face is that this is well beyond our political (with a little "p") time frame based on the next election.

Political with a big "P" is concerned with long-range matters. Consider our energy policy or rather lack it.

The two work together: having a large area means being able to operate at lower intensities of timber harvesting. Intensity is expressed in terms of frequency of successive harvests (cutting cycle or rotation) and the proportion of stand removed in any single harvest operation.

Our hypothetical example: 250,000 acres of suitable forest stands (the net area of, say, a gross suitable area of 400,000 acres, which in turn could be part of an over all forest area of, say 1.5 million acres). This implies two levels of land use planning. First there would be a designation of a gross suitable productive area leaving the rest for non-extractive management and then a net productive area, which would be divided into management units. In each of these there would be annual areas based on rotation or cutting cycle. Balance is between non-extractive preserved areas and net productive areas.

Geographical information system (GIS) mapping and models ("mapematics") would be used to designate the suitable forest area. An assumed 50-year cutting cycle would be based on growth estimates stand by stand (also a combination of forest stand models and GIS models). As a result we would have 50 annual compartments, each 5000 acres. Each area does not have to be all together in a continuous tract. Most likely it will not be due to topographic, soil and stand conditions. A 5000-acre annual area would be based on stand conditions and the timber supply required to sustain a forest industry complex. This is for the sake of example. In reality the area might be larger or smaller.

This accounts for one aspect of intensity: frequency. The other aspect is the proportion of standing timber removed in the annual compartment, which would be determined by stand conditions, mainly growing stock needed to get the next harvest in 50 years in the future. We can assume, for the sake of example, that 30% of standing timber is removed expressed in terms of basal area. The rest (70%) is the growing stock.

So as a result we have a removal intensity of 30% of the stand every 50 years. The forest ecosystem has 50 years to grow back. It may require additional treatment, possibly in the form of thinning.

The idea is to first get to what is referred to as normal stocking (not too thick, not too sparse) and then to keep it in that range through the combination of cutting cycle and harvest proportion. The first step is to be willing to do this and to work on research and development and economics. Finally, this should be a part of our long-range energy portfolio.

Forest health, industry and renewable energy: Part 4

The Taos News – Natural Resources Notebook, April 21 – 27, 2011. p. B10

Wood based renewable energy on a significant scale can be a reality if we get to where we are able to treat large areas of forest based on a sustainable multi-product and service forest industry. Is this wishful thinking? Is it only a dream?

Large areas of healthy forest kept at normal stocking (not too thick, not too sparse) have a great energy potential. Forest acts like huge solar panels converting solar energy to chemical energy through photosynthesis, the process in which carbon dioxide (CO_2) is taken from the atmosphere and turned into carbohydrates, which in turn go to cellulose and other materials in woody tissues. Energy is stored in chemical form in woody tissues to be used whenever needed. So to speak, the batteries are included ("Batteries included: Another angle to solar energy" in The Taos News, Natural Resources Notebook, Nov. 18 - 24, 2010).

What if we decided to use a relatively small portion, say 10%, of our forests for renewable energy? What would that eventually represent in our energy portfolio? We can consider two general categories of energy use: electricity and liquid fuels. Both can make use of wood. Wood-based electricity generation is a reality in some places. At present the economics are not in favor of this option, due to the relatively low cost of fossil fuels. However, if we value environmental services and dangers (oil spills, nuclear accidents and waste disposal) this should at some point tip the balance of renewable sources. Solar and wind are the most commonly known and appreciated new forms of renewable energy (hydroelectric has been around for a long time). Wood-based renewable energy is hardly mentioned in the media and political circles. When it is mentioned it is usually made clear (almost while apologizing) that only wood scraps and waste would be used.

A devil's advocate might say that forest energy means cutting down our forests for fuel. On the contrary, sustainably harvesting growth means improving the health of the forests involved.

     FOREST POWER Adventures in Ecology and Forest Management

Why not seriously declare sustainable productive forest management as a potential major source of energy? A forest taken to and kept at normal stocking is a healthy productive forest that lasts forever. In doing so it not only provides raw material for energy, it removes carbon from the atmosphere (carbon neutrality if burned for energy), releases oxygen, provides water, habitat for wildlife and other benefits while at the same time providing much needed jobs, business opportunities and revenue. Forest management and industry have a large economic multiplier effect from work in the woods to the final consumer or beneficiary.

Our present electrical energy portfolio is something like 50% fossil fuels, maybe 25% hydroelectric, 20% nuclear and less than 5% renewable non-hydroelectric. In 50 years could this look more like 50% renewable, including forest power? What intermediate goals can we set in meantime? (See "An Energy Source Analysis Model" The Taos News, Natural Resources Notebook. Oct 23 – 29 and Nov. 6 – 12, 2008)

The first step is to be willing to seriously consider forests as a sustainable desirable source of environmental friendly energy, while at the same time giving our economy and job situation a boost. Keeping in mind that the idea is to have a balance between productive and non-extractive forest management, and that the forest ecosystems' responses will be monitored, why not work on this?

Considering the present slow job recovery and interest in renewable energy, we would think that politicians and decision-makers would include SPFM on our public forests.

Forest health, industry, renewable energy and jobs: Part 5

The Taos News – Natural Resources Notebook. May 5 – 11, 2011. p. B12

When we get to where forest power is a significant part of our renewable energy portfolio, we will find that its contribution to jobs, business opportunities and revenue made it all the more attractive. We will have been convinced that sustainable productive forest management for energy, wood products and environmental or ecosystem services is truly environmental friendly and is a worthwhile economic development endeavor.

A combination of energy and wood product industry will enable us to treat large areas of forest. As a result we will have a much better balance between our preserved forests on one hand and healthy productively managed forest areas on the other.

Is all this wishful thinking? Is it only a dream? Was getting to the moon in a single decade just a dream?

First of all going from present over-stocked, too thick, unhealthy forest conditions to "just right" (normal stocking) will involve work of many sorts. Work in preparing areas for treatment involves a wide variety of tasks that require a range of skills. There is a great opportunity for our young people and for workers needing to re-train from obsolescent jobs to new skills. The great outdoors offers challenging careers and also step-up jobs in getting to the more technical areas.

Work needed in the woods offers a wide range of business opportunities from very small family businesses with just a couple of chainsaws and a small truck and *ganas de trabajar* to more specialized timber harvesting activities that require costly equipment. Tasks such as marking areas and trees for harvesting and laying out roads in such a way as to not damage soils, don't involve much capital investment. They mostly require skills that can be developed with little equipment.

On the forest industry side there is a wide range of skills and educational requirements. The research and development needed offers great opportunities.

"We had a dream" may be a reality in time. What if, in 50 years, a Rip Van Winkle woke up to a scenario in which 20% of our forest area was sustainably producing energy making up 10% of our renewable energy portfolio and in which a large workforce is permanently involved in the endeavor? And this is production that can't be outsourced.

Of course we can't do it all at once. We have to start with deciding that it's worth doing; that it's worth trying. We could designate pilot areas for treatment, which would be closely monitored by a range of environmental organizations.

At present it would seem that private forests will have to lead the way and show that sustainable productive forest management is really sustainable; that certain forests can be managed in such a way as to harvest growth without damaging forest ecosystems. "Certain forests" means that they have topographic, soil and stand characteristics that make it viable. Just in designating such forests we will find that we end up with a balance between productively managed forests and those that remain preserved under sustainable non-extractive management.

Going from our present electrical energy portfolio with less than 5% renewable sources to a healthier energy environment will generate jobs. The forest component will take time but it will come of age. In doing so we will discover the enormous potential of forest power.

Are we willing to seriously consider forests as a sustainable desirable source of environmental friendly energy? Why not?

We must get over the taboo of logging and what might be referred to as the "Spotted Owl syndrome". Our efforts should be focused on forest ecosystems and not individual trees. Spotted Owls and other wildlife can co-exist with timber harvesting, yes cutting trees!, in SPFM. Provisions can be made for habitat in SPFM and further enhanced with a balance with SNEFM. It's not a choice between wildlife and the energy-products-jobs combo. We can have both in balance and that will enhance over all sustainability.

In order to have a forest industry that in turn will enable us to have large scale forest treatment, we must be willing to consider logging (timber harvesting) as a term and more important, as a concept.

LOGGING – TIMBER HARVESTING

Logging or timber harvesting is a major component in SPFM. But it should not be considered outside of the context of the framework of sustainable management. It's one of many operations and, when done under adequate forest regulation, it should be considered a silvicultural treatment that is part of the over all productive management system. We must understand that a system is made up of components that work together resulting a pattern of behavior, often in response to external stimulae. Silvicultural systems are built around timber harvesting, which in turn is based on silvics (forest ecology). So what's wrong with logging?

What's wrong with logging?

The Taos News – Natural Resources Notebook. Dec 23 - 29, 2010. p. B6

It would seem that using the word "logging" is not politically correct. Why not? Is it a bad word? This is not about logging on to your e-mail or bank account website on the Internet. It's about an operation that is a part of sustainable productive forest management (SPFM).

Is it the word or the process? Would calling it something like "Habitat for Bambi" (or restoration) help?

Logging is timber harvesting. A logger is one who is involved in the process of harvesting trees that have been designated for such by forestry multidisciplinary teams that include wildlife biologists, ecologists, forest managers, soils specialists and others. This is the case when timber harvesting is part of a much larger picture: SPFM. Loggers or logging companies do not decide which trees are to be removed. That is the job of professional foresters working in an interdisciplinary team and following policy guidelines. Management planning, like any management venture, is objective-oriented. Usually, almost always, there is more than one objective. The planning process is multi-objective in which certain objectives have priority and determine restrictions that must be placed on achieving secondary objectives. An example would be SPFM on a watershed. The main objective is water production. Any other treatments must be compatible with the water producing capacity of the watershed forest ecosystems.

Removal of trees from the ecosystem is done by nature through natural mortality, fire, wind, disease and insects. Trees are "lost". The forest ecosystem responds by having new trees born, younger, smaller trees can grow to replace of those removed. This is all part of forest ecosystem dynamics. Human involvement in the process can be productive. Trees removed are converted to wood products and energy, for example. The process of such removal: logging. Timber harvesting is the series of often highly specialized operations that get the wood (timber) from the stump to the mill. It's dangerous work, which can be appreciated by reviewing employer workers comp insurance rates. They are comparable to mining and deep-sea commercial fishing as done off the coasts of Alaska, for example.

Is it that much different from the operation in which plants are harvested to provide our daily bread? Is a wheat plant a lowly being compared to a tree? Why? True, one difference is that wheat plants are planted, cultivated. Trees often are too. "Cultivation" can be through actual tree planting using stock from nurseries or it can be through natural means. Foresters call the latter "natural regeneration". Often timber harvesting is done in such a way as to enhance natural regeneration. Silvicultural systems are designed around that in SPFM where ecosystem resilience plays a major role.

Establishing trees after timber harvesting (sometimes before) can be through natural regeneration or planting. In natural regeneration the conditions are created for the forest to regenerate on its own. This is what silvicultural systems are about.

The bottom line: logging can be good for the environment in helping to have healthier forests. Room to grow is healthy condition while too thick is not. It can also enhance biodiversity by improving habitat diversity by making varying sizes of small open spaces that are good for grass and brush for wildlife. And, furthermore, it can provide much-need sustainable jobs and revenue. "Is logging good for the environment?" was published in the "Forum" section of The Taos News, September 23, 2004. (www.cmb-lwv.com.ve/is_logging_good.htm)

Once treatment has been undertaken, whether it's considered (or called) restoration or under sustainable productive forest management (SPFM) principles, the forest ecosystem's response must be continuously evaluated (monitored) in order to compare real results with those predicted in the management plans. Multi-party monitoring is an essential ingredient for sustainability and credibility.

FOREST MANAGEMENT MONITORING

Monitoring and credibility

The Taos News – Natural Resources Notebook. Nov 1 - 7, 2007

Can we trust the mouse to watch over the cheese? The mouse may be honest, but it may have a credibility problem.

What is monitoring? What does it mean to monitor something? I am sure that most people have a good idea how to answer these questions. A more challenging question however, would be, "What is the role of monitoring in the management of natural resources?"

A major part of natural resource management is the decision-making process. Some choices include how a natural resource should be used, what are the expected results of use (costs and benefits), or whether a natural resource should even be exploited. Once the decision has been made to utilize a natural resource, for example the rather controversial act of harvesting timber in a national forest, the public must be informed as to the methods by which the forest managers will proceed with the harvesting and how it fits into the context of sustainable management. Such subsequent decisions will include harvest intensity (amount of timber removed at a given time), rotation or "cutting cycle" (length of time between harvests), and the restrictions that should be imposed to protect or sustain other forest uses. As an example, the forest manager may ask what size, age, species, and location of trees would benefit an endangered species such as the spotted owl or what type of cutting will have the least impact on soil erosion. These types of decisions are necessary to achieve sustainability in a forest setting.

Information is the main input for achieving competent decisions. It is important to know how similar managerial actions with respect to natural resources that were implemented in the past have affected entire ecosystems and individual components of ecosystems. For the information to be useful in future projects, the data must have been gathered in a systematic and unbiased manner, recording all results whether desirable or undesirable. This data-gathering process is what we define as "monitoring." The monitoring of natural resources should be done not only by the governmental agency involved (i.e., in our example, the Forest Service), but also by concerned non-governmental organizations. Multi-participatory monitoring could lessen the credibility gap often encountered when sensitive environmental issues are involved. Sustainability supported by trust-worthy monitoring is not only ecologically, technologically, and economically desirable, but socially desirable, i.e., obtaining strong public support for responsible managerial actions.

In order that the independent monitors as well as the governmental agencies maintain the highest levels of credibility, all persons involved should be well educated in the monitoring process and in basic ecology and elements of resource management. On occasion, even the best intentions of those trying to preserve and protect our natural resources can yield unexpected and deleterious results if the monitors have not been well educated. This solid education in the monitoring and scientific data gathering processes also applies to the governmental agencies who work with the independent agencies. Well-intended but ultimately misguided, poorly educated efforts are, in the end, counterproductive.

The bottom line: Well-prepared and well-educated multi-party monitors who work cooperatively can enhance the credibility of the monitoring process as well as improve the overall management of the natural resource.

Special thanks to Debbie Ragland, UNM-Taos geology, for her valuable contribution in reviewing and editing.

Credibility: This what is lacking on the part of the general public regarding forest managers. This is why there is so much pressure to impose or implement simplistic largely ineffective and often counter-productive measures such as just leave-it-alone or a size cap on trees to be removed in forest treatment.

Management, the public and credibility

The Taos News – Natural Resources Notebook. July 17 – 23, 2008. p. C8

Well-intentioned efforts by environmental activists can often be counter productive in public forest management.

When public forest managers decide to carry out an action such as timber harvesting (logging), they are often confronted with opposition from groups who feel that they need to second-guess forest officials. For example, a timber sale may be part of an overall strategy and management plan, having been developed by groups of professionals and subjected to public opinion, and still when it is to be implemented, groups of well-intentioned people try to block it. A basic underlying problem here is credibility. The groups who oppose the action may not be, and probably aren't as knowledgeable as the forest managers, but the activists don't believe in them. Taking measures to block a well-planned, ecologically sound treatment that is to be undertaken in the framework of sustainable forest management would be like a group of passengers on a plane going into the flight deck and blocking the pilots and navigators from doing their job of flying the plane. The end results could be quite different from those intended by the flight activists, who in this example, think they know more than the pilots.

Public awareness and participation is desirable and necessary. Credibility of forest managers will be enhanced by effective public involvement in the planning, execution and specially monitoring of management actions such as timber harvesting. We must emphasize the word "effective". Effectiveness and desired outcomes will depend on the activist's knowledge and understanding of basic forest ecology and management principles. Similarly public monitoring of aviation safety is necessary. Obviously those who would suggest improvements to aviation experts, pilots and airline administrators have to know quite about flying, navigation, airplane maintenance and airline administration.

When watchdog groups of activists take actions without having the basic knowledge or hiring the necessary expertise, they are assuming that the public forest managers are either incompetent (in the best of cases) or corrupt or just plain crooked. This means that, in the eyes of activists, foresters and other professionals are sold out to special interests contrary to the well being of the forest and sustainability of forest management. This is the credibility problem.

One thing that we all must be aware of is that forest ecosystems respond to alterations of various sorts, such as fire or even clear-cutting. They are complex living entities that have survived all sorts of calamities, both natural and human. Their resilience lies in the complex interactions among living organisms, plant and animal, small and large, that have proven effective over long periods of time, even before the emergence of humans and our impacts on our environment. We must appreciate that a given event, be it fire or, again, our clear-cutting example, may at first (just after the fire or logging) look horrible and seem to be a total disaster. If we watch the area during the years following the event, we will see the forest ecosystem responding, "healing its wounds" so to speak. A geographically broad forest ecosystem includes plants that are in charge of covering the ground taking advantage of the new conditions, such as open sunlight, to get established. They pave the way for other plants providing a favorable microclimate. What we will be experiencing is ecological succession. Forest ecologists and managers use natural means often helped along with "artificial" means such as seeding or planting. We can refer to the "right now" versus the "later" regarding response of the forest ecosystem as apparent impact vs. real impact of an alteration. What really matters is the real impact that is the result of the forest ecosystem's response to the event.

Enlightened, knowledgeable environmental activists would best serve the public's interest by taking an active positive approach in participating in the planning of forest treatments such as timber harvesting and assuming a "let's do it" approach while committing themselves to a more patient "wait and see" stance in which they will be directly involved in the "seeing" process (monitoring).

An area submitted to timber harvest, a prescribed burn (which also may look terrible at first) or a fire should be monitored by both forest managers and environmental activists. Monitoring should include all possible practical aspects including soil erosion through sediment monitoring as well as the actual forest response. Biodiversity will be affected at first so monitoring this aspect of the response is important. Likewise the effects on wildlife should be considered as well as aesthetic values.

Public awareness and activism is an important element of natural resource management and must be guided by solid knowledge of basic forest ecology supported by expertise in other aspects such as the economics of forest management practices, logging, engineering and information science.

We often hear about how our public forests were over-cut and seriously deteriorated in the 80's. It would be wise to take a look at some of them and see how the forest ecosystems have responded. We may be surprised! Demo areas should be set up or designated, evaluated and monitored to find out, objectively, if indeed they were permanently harmed. Was the so-called market-driven over cutting bad? Might it not have been bad? Maybe even good?

Demo areas in forest treatment monitoring

The Taos News – Natural Resources Notebook. Sep 23 - 29, 2010. p. B5

Have past forest harvesting (logging) practices been good or bad? Demonstration areas can show how forest ecosystems are resilient.

Forest ecosystems are living entities and as such react to what happens to them and to their habitat. Response to alterations of different intensities is part of their inherent capabilities that have evolved over long periods of time as a means of survival. That's what resiliency means. In general it can be said that species such as our ponderosa pine, blue spruce or aspen have found ways to survive a wide range of catastrophes. Probably the most common is fire. Going further in our thinking, individual genetic makeup wants to survive in individuals and in their associations in communities of living things, in ecosystems. Our genes and those of trees want to perpetuate themselves through survival and reproduction.

So what happens when an apparently destructive event like fire happens to a forest: Is it lost forever? The answer is no, or else there wouldn't be any forests. Forests regenerate themselves through a wide variety of mechanisms. The bottom line is ecosystem resiliency, closely associated with soil health and biodiversity.

A picture is worth a hundred words and a real-life setting is worth a hundred pictures. Multi-party monitoring, or for that matter any monitoring, requires training, which can be in the form of written and verbal communication supported by real situations where one can see, feel, hear, smell the forest setting. In living and appreciating such an experience, knowledge of the history of that particular forest stand is a must. Wouldn't it be good if we had a set of forest demonstration areas ranging from undisturbed forests to the most altered situations imaginable (intense fire, clearcutting)? Maybe we do have this but if so, it's not well known to the general public.

Undisturbed areas should be easy to find in our Carson National Forest and privately owned forests in the area. Finding documented altered areas is a more difficult matter. We know about areas where timber harvesting took place years ago. It would be good to be able to see these areas 50 years later. We could see how each forest ecosystem has responded to, for instance, possible over-cutting. This would include observing soil conditions as well as forest stands. We would be looking for regeneration (new born trees) and health and growth of surviving trees, some of which may have been scarred during harvesting.

To get the most out of this we would need to know what the stand was like before treatment (logging) took place. We would also need to know how much timber was removed and how much of the remaining stand was damaged by the logging process. Finally it would be great to know what the remaining stand was like. Describing what it was like involves qualitative information regarding number of trees per acre, their distribution by size (diameter classes) and the basal area of the stand. Basal area is the sum of the cross-sections taken at 4.5 feet height on the trunk, calculated from measuring diameter (DBH).

In an ITTO project in Venezuelan tropical forests, we proposed what we called the "pre-post" forest monitoring model using a combination of one-time (static) inventories (temporary plot samples) and dynamic sampling using permanent plots that can be measured periodically.

Retroactive monitoring is not simple but it's needed for evaluation and for public credibility in sustainable productive forest management.

Demo areas should also be monitored regarding the possible impacts on wildlife. This is another angle in the evaluation of forest treatment practices. We will only consider one aspect here, that of wildlife corridors.

WILDLIFE AND FOREST MANAGEMENT

Can wildlife corridors and productive forest management co-exist?

The Taos News – Natural Resources Notebook. Nov 4 - 10, 2010. p. B7

Large wild animals, such as elk, need to be able to move around over significant distances in order to sustain their way of living. Wildlife corridors are designed to enable them to move without barriers that they can't handle. This is a major concern in large-scale land use planning. A corridor must have a diverse range of habitats within it to provide cover, food and water. What human activities are compatible with corridors? Timber harvesting or logging is one to consider.

First of all timber harvesting must be seen as part of a bigger picture: sustainable productive forest management (SPFM). The sustainable part has to do with regulating cutting (timber harvesting) so that it's limited to the amount of growth that takes pace, which must be continuously monitored. Second it involves taking measures to ensure that soil and biodiversity are not damaged. Third it involves the economics and politics that make the whole operation sustainable in the long run, meaning forever.

Timber harvesting is the process of extracting wood from the forest for products and energy. Loggers only take out what forest managers designate and in the way that foresters determine, which means that they must do it in such a way as not to do permanent harm to the ecosystem, mainly the forest soil.

Long-term management plans are developed by Interdisciplinary teams that, besides foresters, include, among other specialties, wildlife biologists who can specify the kind of habitat diversity that is best for animals of all species in or associated with a forest ecosystem. Habitat diversity sets the basis for the variety of cover, food and water that everything from squirrels to bears (and spotted owls) need.

Forest ecosystems that make up part of the corridors are naturally diverse. Elements such as fire help to achieve this diversity. However in certain cases (maintaining a balance) it may be desirable to help nature along and enhance habitat diversity through a range of forest treatment practices, while at the same time producing water, jobs and other benefits. Silvicultural practices are designed to achieve objectives, whatever they may be. Here the predominant objective would be wildlife through sustainable corridors and water (watersheds). Usually we will be considering a basket of uses and environmental services (objectives): water, wildlife, wood products, recreation, improved atmosphere (CO2 and O2).

Now, how would SPFM affect a wildlife corridor? To answer the question, first we need to understand SPFM, especially regarding its intensity in time and in place. The cutting cycle or rotation is the main factor. On relatively slow-growing forests such as we have in northern New Mexico and southern Colorado, a cutting cycle might be as long as 50 years or more. This is the time between timber harvesting (logging) operations. It allows the forest to recover based on forest ecosystems' natural resilience. The other main matter is harvest intensity at a given time. These two "levers" let foresters regulate the rate of removal to accommodate the forest ecosystem's ability to regenerate and grow. It's a little like a savings account where we "harvest" only the interest without affecting the capital, while at the same time taking care of the "bank" and the community.

Can wildlife corridors and logging co-exist? Yes, provided that adequate biological and ecological based measures are taken. Timber harvesting within the framework of sustainable productive forest management can actually improve wildlife corridors through habitat diversity enhancement.

The discussion on forest management and the balance between SPFM and SNEFM is applicable to forest areas where water resources are the main objective. This leads us in our adventure to the fascinating world of watersheds.

WATERSHEDS

Water is vital for all life as we know it. We can appreciate it but do we? It's the ultimate commodity (you can live longer without food than without water) and it's one that is rapidly becoming a major international concern. In thinking about water we must consider watersheds and their associated forests in most of them.

Where does our water come from?

The Taos News – Natural Resources Notebook. July 3 – 9, 2008. p. B11

Can we improve our watersheds?

For generations our area's *acequia* systems have been the lifeblood of rural living and a cultural heritage treasure. Water is a critical natural resource in our area and southwest region in general due to its importance (everywhere) and its scarcity (here). The more scarce a resource is the more valuable it becomes. As population and economic activity grow, so does the demand for water. Where does our water come from? The answer brings on another question. How far back or how deep do we want to go in our thinking? The earth was "born" with a finite amount of water (though we possibly get a tiny bit from meteors) which has its origin in the solar system and beyond. Water is made of hydrogen and oxygen, the latter generated through nuclear fusion in massive stars that preceded our sun's formation (the sun is our closest star). Fortunately this combination of hydrogen and oxygen is stable. It goes through solid, liquid and gaseous states without changing its composition. It's always H2O. We'll leave the chemistry and astrophysics at this point and move on to our thinking in terms of natural resources, their importance, use and management.

The water for our acequias comes from our watersheds which act as giant sponges that soak up atmospheric water (rain, dew and snow) and gradually release it in our mountain streams. Most watersheds are covered to a large extent by forests which play a major role in the "sponge effect". The "sponge" is a combination of vegetation, animals and soil. Soil, along with climate and topography (altitude, slope and aspect), is a determining factor in the vegetation. Climate, soil and topography make up the habitat of the forest. Vegetation, specifically the forest, can be manipulated by human intervention through management practices such as thinning.

The idea behind this discussion is to consider watershed management in the context of natural resource management. The main concern is sustainability which is vital to our survival. One consideration is whether to protect or actively manage a watershed (protection is also a form of management). In the first case we must be aware that protection may not guarantee sustainability. Let's consider a forested watershed which could be any of ours in the area. I would like to consider San Cristobal not only because it's my home but because it is small enough to be taken as a sort of model. Red River or Hondo would be much more complicated due to size and also human complications since they are inhabited watersheds. We can think of the watershed as a "producing area" and, in our model, the San Cristobal valley as a "consuming area".

In watershed management, as in any other resource, we start by formulating policy, objectives and goals and develop a management plan. Generally speaking we have two main elements to consider. The first is managing the vegetation, meaning a form of forest management. The second is the possibility of engineering structures to regulate flow (dams and releases) or by stabilizing erosion-prone areas which require geologic and engineering expertise and money. We will concentrate on the forest management aspect. What could we do to maintain stream flow or even increase it? Sustainability demands a healthy forest, so the first consideration is trying to keep the forest healthy. Thinning can be done for forest health and also possibly to increase stream flow or at least regulate it through manipulation of the snow pack. One of the effects of trees is to intercept snow fall in the crowns, which increases the amount of snow lost to sublimation (solid state to gaseous state) before it can accumulate as snow pack. Theoretically we can have a better snow pack by not having too thick a forest. On the other hand, a forest that is too sparse will expose more of the snow pack to sunlight and, again, result in loss. There should be an optimum forest density that will maximize the amount of snow retained to feed the streams and our acequias.

A major difficulty is that much of our watershed forest is pretty much inaccessible for thinning. The economics of it are going against us. It simply costs too much. However, how much is water worth? Think of the Lama watershed and the effect of the Hondo fire. Could something have been done in forest management to mitigate the damage, to reduce the intensity of the fire, even before it got to the Lama watershed? Or might the fire possibly improve water production later on. Again, there are no easy answers.

What is a watershed?

The Taos News – Natural Resources Notebook. Sep 17 - 23, 2009. p. B7

What is a watershed? We see the term often, but do we really appreciate the full meaning and, more important, especially in our Northern Rio Grande region, what its significance is to people that have lived here for centuries. Water is vital and scarcity makes it more so throughout the southwest. Where does the water in our streams or wells come from? The answer: our watersheds.

Think of a watershed as a basin that catches precipitation (rain and snow) and channels it to a place from where it runs somewhere and is used by some things, including people. It's like a roof with gutters that lead to a tank. This literally could be a shed! Also "shed" could be from the verb "to shed". An area sheds water as it falls on it.

Imagine a large structure with a tin roof. What happens when it rains? The water rushes off the roof. Very little remains on the roof surface due to the "sticking power" of water. That quickly dries out meaning that it evaporates back into the air. Now let's imagine a very special roof on our structure. We'll stick sponges all over its surface. Now what happens when it rains? Obviously some of the water is retained, soaked up by the sponge layer. The rest runs off the roof once the sponges are "full". We could think in terms of a water budget. Water goes into them until they are saturated, then it runs off the roof. Some of the water retained in the sponge layer evaporates back into the atmosphere. Eventually the sponge layer will lose most of the water, maybe all of it if there is a long enough time without more rain.

Now let's complicate things. We'll add more sponge over the surface of our tin roof but not uniformly. We'll make it diverse. We'll make it thicker in some places. In others we'll use a different kind of sponge. What we have done is make a "model" of a watershed.

Now, what is our "sponge" in a real watershed? Obviously it's much more complex. It's supposed to be that way since a model by definition is a simplification of reality. In a nutshell it's soil and vegetation on a given topography. This living and non-living "sponge" is very complex and diverse. Different rock formations lead to different soils, which, along with altitude, slope and aspect, in turn lead to different types of vegetation. Look at any specific watershed in our area, the smaller the better it is to understand it. Two factors stand out: altitude and aspect. How high up the canyon are we? In which direction does the slope face? (Aspect) The higher, the cooler and wetter (or less dry) it is. The more a slope is shaded from the sun, the cooler it is and, again more moist. Add slope and soil type to the equation to appreciate its diversity. As a result forest types are diverse. We have scrub oak, pinyon-juniper and ponderosa pine at lower altitudes and spruce-fir at higher altitudes. Add events such as fire to further complicate the matter. Where spruce-fir has burned we often have aspen. Where ponderosa has burned we often get oak, but first a lot of grass and shrubs.

What defines the borders or the spatial extent of our watershed? The answer: topography, ridges. More next time.

Watersheds and water budgets

The Taos News – Natural Resources Notebook. Oct 1 – 7, 2009. p. B6

A watershed can be said to have a water budget. What we are most familiar with is what comes out and feeds our *acequias* and aquifers that in turn feed our wells, while what's left over runs further downstream for other users in other areas.

What is a water budget? It could have to do with our water bills, but that's not where we're going here. A budget is a balance between what comes in and what goes out of something. An example could be a flowerpot. We put water in and some water comes out, usually into a plate under the pot. If we knew exactly how much water the soil in the pot can retain and how much the flower plant uses and loses (through evapotranspiration), we could add just the right amount of water and not have any draining out. Usually we don't know this, so we add water as we feel it's needed. This is an example of a soil water budget in a small "system". Now, we'll consider a much larger system: a watershed.

In order to apply the reasoning based on a system, we have to have a clear definition of what the system is, mainly its boundaries (what's included and what's not). What defines the borders or the spatial extent of a watershed? How do we separate one watershed from another? The answer: topography, basically ridges. Just like the peak of a two-sided pitched roof, a ridge determines which way water flows. It marks a line that separates water flow in two different directions. So a complex of connected ridges determines the limits, the borders of a watershed.

A watershed is usually associated with a stream or river. It can be small like our San Cristobal watershed. The Rio Grande watershed is large made up of a vein-like network of tributaries, each with its own watershed.

Once we have defined a specific watershed, we can think of the dynamics of it in terms of a water budget. How much water enters the watershed in the form of rain, snow or dew? We assume that there is no aquifer that brings water in from an adjacent watershed. This probably is valid but we can't be sure unless we know the geology of the area very well. How much water leaves the watershed? This would be the flow of the stream plus phreatic water (shallow ground water) associated with the stream, evaporation and, again, maybe an aquifer that feeds from somewhere in the watershed and then shows up somewhere else. What goes on inside the watershed? How much water is stored? For how long? This will determine a sort of time lag. In general, the longer the time lag the more stable the stream flow, meaning less variation due to climatic cycles, droughts in our case in Northern NM. This leads to considering a watershed model.

What we are doing is considering the watershed as a system and trying to describe it with a model. In systems ecology, dealing with identification and study of systems, we define the system to our convenience and the objectives of the study. In this case we have a well-defined system: our small watershed. We have considered the inputs (water in) and outputs (water out). We have also decided that we are only considering water and not other elements such as nutrients, solar energy, etc. It gets more complicated!

Here, again we'll consider a systems approach in our adventures in ecology and forest management. Watersheds, the places where our water comes from (a ground view of the hydrologic –water- cycle), are fascinating systems. The complex interactions and dynamics of geology, topography, soils, forests, non-forest vegetation and animals in watershed ecosystems present a challenging area of study.

Think of a watershed as an ecosystem

The Taos News – Natural Resources Notebook. Oct 15 – 21, 2009. p. B7

In the two previous columns we have defined a watershed and considered models starting from a simple tin roof and sponge analogy and going on to considering water budgets in a systems analysis approach. As we said: It gets more complicated!

What we are doing is considering the watershed as a system and trying to describe it with a model. Systems ecology deals with the identification and study of ecosystems through modeling, which involves a complex process of formulating models, testing them by comparing their results to real systems and then adjusting them and further testing in a continuous process. These math and computer models can then be used to experiment: to try to answer "what if ..." questions. For example: What if there is a fire? How does it affect water yield? In this case our system and its model is a small watershed. We have considered the inputs (water in) and outputs (water out) in the form of a budget. We are limiting our model to only considering water leaving out other elements such as nutrients, solar energy, etc., which is a strategy in modeling. Think of a watershed as an ecosystem.

What does a watershed do? It catches and saves water. It "administrates" it. A watershed receives a certain amount of water (input) and distributes it (output). There is a time lag from the moment water enters a watershed and the moment it flows out. Output (outflow) takes places place on the surface, the stream and underground, the latter through a relatively shallow area underneath and along the stream. This is phreatic water. Plants that use it are phreatophytes. This is evident along our acequias, which have developed an associated vegetation (willows and cottonwoods) due to the availability of phreatic water associated with them. Deeper water seepage takes place through aquifers determined by the geology of the watershed. Aquifers are porous rock or sediment layers through which water flows like underground streams.

The major components of a watershed (using a system approach) are: underlying geology, rock formations (the tin roof in our roof and sponge analogy), that determine topography and along with climate finally determine soils; vegetation types including forests, tundra, grasslands (the "sponge"), water (of course), gravity, time and events that cause alterations (fire, landslides).

What causes the time lag? Vegetation, especially forests due to their diverse composition and structure, are a major component of the "sponge effect". The other major component is soil. The combination of soil and vegetation (the sponge) receives water, and gradually releases it. The forest canopy acts as a "shock absorber" reducing the impact of heavy rain. It also intercepts and briefly holds some of the water, especially in the case of snow. Part of it drips to the soil surface and the rest is released back into the atmosphere (output, lost for water users) through evaporation of water or sublimation of snow (solid to gas without going through the liquid form). Therefore forest density is a major variable in determining what happens to water entering the system. This is one aspect that can be modified to a certain extent through forest management.

Even a small watershed is complex. It can be considered as being made up of many sub-systems, each of which can be taken as an ecosystem. It gets even more complicated. Here's another good reason for our high school and college students to acquire math and computer capabilities.

Watershed ecosystems: Part 2

The Taos News – Natural Resources Notebook. Oct 29 – Nov. 4, 2009. p. B5

How can we describe a watershed? We have stated that even a small watershed is quite complex; that it can be considered as being made up of many sub-systems, each of which can be considered an ecosystem in itself.

In characterizing a system of any kind, we tend to break it down into components that we can study and understand better. We can break a watershed into functional components such as underlying rock, soil, litter (not decomposed), organic matter layer, low herb and shrub vegetation and forest including intermediate "layers" (strata; trees by height classes) and the canopy. Or, we can break it down into spatial or geographic units, each of which is made up of rock-topographic type, soil type and forest type. Actually we will most likely use a combination of both approaches. First we break the watershed into forest types or stands that we can identify. Then we consider each in terms of its physical components. Each forest type or stand can be considered an ecosystem depending on the level of detail that we want.

A forest type is a general category, an abstract unit. A forest stand is a specific spatial unit that can be identified, delimited and mapped. A given stand can be said to belong to a forest type. A forest type can appear as a series of forest stands in different locations.

In this approach a major aspect of the effort will be in gathering data. We can imagine a set of data points. The location of each data point is determined in terms of geographic coordinates that can be obtained using a GPS unit (Global Positioning System) or by remote sensing (use of satellite images or aerial photos). As a result the data points can be mapped. Now what we need is a set of characteristics for each data point. For example a point will be associated with a forest type, a topographic type (i.e. elevation, slope, aspect) and a soil type. As a result we will end up with quite a lot of data for each data point. From this we can make a topographic type map. Then we can have a map of forest types and another for soil types. We can go even further considering forest stand density and fuel load and presence of insect infestations or disease, from which we can develop maps that can give us an idea as to the general health of the forest stand and specific problem areas that we may want to pay particular attention to.

Now, what do we do with all these maps? Say for instance that we want to relate forest stocking level (how thick it is) with insect or disease. We can overlay the maps and establish relationships. A powerful tool for this what is referred to as geographical information systems (GIS). A hypothesis might be that forest stands that are too thick are more likely to have a higher risk of fire or problems with disease and/or insect infestations and that this may be different for different forest types. We can then "test" this hypothesis using statistical analysis in combination with the GIS application. In the end the implication is that we are thinking of doing something about it. Hence the use of converting raw data into information and establishing conclusions that can guide watershed treatment.

For our students: explore a fascinating world of math, computer applications, geography and natural resources in GIS.

Soils: A component of watershed ecosystems: Part 3

The Taos News – Natural Resources Notebook. Nov 12 – 18, 2009. p. B6

Forests and other types of vegetation are probably what first comes to mind when we describe a watershed ecosystem but what determines what kind of vegetation we have in a given location?

So far in the last three columns we have concentrated on the forest element of watersheds in thinking of them as ecosystems or a set of ecosystems that make up a given watershed. We have considered breaking the watershed ecosystem into its components, mostly in terms of forest types. There are other non-forest ecosystems in most of our northern New Mexico watersheds. If we look around as we drive through the Hondo or Red River canyons or as we walk up any of our smaller canyons, we see areas of almost solid rock. At first glance it might appear that there is no soil or vegetation, but if we look closely we'll see traces of both in cracks and crevices; on small ledges and in anyplace that can catch and gather material loosened by weathering. And in many of these we'll see some form of plants and even tiny animals.

So this time we'll start from scratch in considering how different ecosystems develop in a watershed. Soil doesn't just happen. It doesn't just exist. Soils evolve from solid rock or from deposits of relatively loose rock fragments, pieces that are transported by gravity (falling and rolling), by water or finer grains by wind. Soil is "produced" by nature from solid rock or from these deposits. Climate, vegetation and time combine their efforts to build the soil that supports forests. Soil and vegetation together make up the "sponge" that we have referred to in our analogy of how a watershed "administrates" water. Soils along with climate and topography make up the physical habitat in which trees and other plants in the living component of the ecosystems live. An ecosystem is made up of habitat and the communities of living things.

So soil is a component of the ecosystem. What is soil? Is it soil or dirt? Have you ever heard of "dirt science"? Generally speaking, soil is the stuff that plants and forests grow in. Dirt is, well, dirty! We should not use the term "soiled" clothes when we mean "dirty" clothes. The scientific field that deals with soils is soil science.

Understanding the soil is a must in understanding a forest ecosystem in a watershed. Soils are described in terms of their physical and chemical properties. Texture, the proportions of sand, silt and clay, and structure, how particles stick together (having to do with clods) are the main physical properties. Chemical properties have to do with mineral nutrients in the soil. Organic matter (humus) content is a major attribute of soils, which is what we see when we scrape the surface of a forest soil.

What can we do about soil in a watershed? Usually very little. The main thing is to try to keep from losing it though erosion. Actually we should say keep loss at a minimum since some erosion is natural and inevitable. To a certain degree we can assert an effect through forest stand management by thinning and deadwood management (removal of natural debris, possibly by prescribed burning or wood gathering).

For our students, consider a field of study in soil science involving physics, chemistry, geology and ecology with applications in natural resources, environmental science and engineering (buildings, roads and bridges are built on soils).

Watershed management is closely related to SPFM and SNEFM. Here, non-extractive (the "NE" part of the acronym) should be changed to non-manipulative, since modifications can be made without actually extracting anything. An example would be non-extractive thinning to optimize snow-packs or engineering structures to mitigate streamside erosion. The principles involved are the same or similar. The bottom line is that management is objective oriented, where there usually is more than a single dominant objective, which in the case of watersheds obviously is water as an environmental service and commodity.

A look at active and non-active watershed management

The Taos News – Natural Resources Notebook. Dec 3 – 9, 2009. p. B5

What is watershed management? There are things we can do to protect our watersheds and there are things we can do to enhance water production. It depends on what our objectives are, the technology and resources available and the political will of the public. "Management" implies that there be a clearly defined set of objectives set forth within a pre-established policy framework. It does not mean that the ecosystem has to be altered in any way.

Obviously the main objective is to "produce" water in sufficient quantity and quality. An example of policy would be that the watershed is not to be purposely altered. It's still management. The fact that the area has to be under some form of administration to ensure protection: law enforcement and decisions on fire control, qualifies the undertaking as management. A contrasting policy would be that actions be taken to improve either quantity or quality of the water. The "owners", usually the public through agencies, make the policy, or it may be set forth in laws and regulations.

Watershed management is based on a sufficient degree of understanding of a watershed ecosystem; in short on information, which is input for decision-making. There is a wide range of sources of information. Existing knowledge and tradition, especially significant in our acequia culture is an example. On the higher end of the technological nature of sources, we have mentioned the use of geographical information systems (GIS) and complex computer models to evaluate options. The implication here is that we might consider some form of forest stand treatment to improve our watershed.

We might want to consider a hypothesis to the effect that forest stands that are too thick are more likely to have a higher risk of fire or problems with disease and/or insect infestations and that this may be different for different forest types and stands. We can then "test" this hypothesis using statistical analysis in combination with the GIS application. In the end the implication is that we are thinking of doing something about it. Hence the use of converting raw data into information and establishing conclusions that can guide watershed treatment.

"Active" watershed management can be approached from two angles: one is through manipulation of the forest cover, mainly by thinning; the other is from an structural engineering perspective involving stream course stabilization, retention walls, and even dams. "Active" management means that the watershed is manipulated in some form with certain objectives in mind. These usually are water flow stabilization and in some cases manipulating forest canopy density to increase total output. Non-active ("passive"?) management would be conserving some form of status quo, accepting what the watershed produces without trying to modify it. Basically this means trying to maintain the watershed through fire control and limitations on human use of the watershed.

In general, a healthy watershed means being made up of healthy forests and other vegetation types. Though it's usually impractical to achieve healthy forest conditions in the whole watershed, we can consider creating and maintaining a healthy forest buffer zone around critical areas. "Healthy" is not easy to define, but a major aspect is that the forest not be too thick (it should have room to grow) nor have too much deadwood accumulation so that it is more resistant to fire, insect damage and disease. Bio-diversity and structural and spatial diversity are other aspects.

Up to here our adventures have been in ecology basics, principles and application of sustainable productive forest management (SPFM) in balance with sustainable non-extractive forest management (SNEFM), passing through consideration of forest biomass as a sustainable renewable source of energy; and watersheds. Any kind of management involves planning, testing "what if" scenarios, monitoring and evaluating, all of which make use of math, especially in models. Decision-making and information science are closely related. Ecosystem modeling, systems ecology, is part of decision science involving management information systems, which again use math and computer models to test "what-if's". What if we do such and such? What if we don't? How do the forest ecosystems respond to a given treatment of management regime? How do they behave if nothing is done (meaning no extractive or alteration treatment, however light or heavy)?

So, logically, now we'll have a brief excursion into the use of math in ecology and forest management.

MATH IN FORESTRY: SYSTEM MODELS AND STATISTICS

Math in forestry

The Taos News – Natural Resources Notebook. Aug 20 – 26, 2009. p. B11

Why study math if you're going to be an outdoor's person? When I started forestry school at CSU in 1959, I didn't want to spend time studying math and other basics. I wanted forestry courses!

So what good is math for working in forestry? To start with, any decision that has to be made has to be based on information. For example: How many trees are there per acre? How thick is the forest in terms of basal area?

Another important aspect: How fast is the forest stand changing? Rate of change is part of the dynamics of forest ecosystems. How fast do trees grow? How fast does the forest stand become thicker? Rates of change involve math, all the way from simple linear equations like $Y = a + bX$, to complex systems of differential equations.

How do foresters answer these questions? We can't go out and measure all the trees even in a relatively small forest, say around 25 acres. What do we do? We take a sample made up of plots in each of which we count and measure the trees. But then how good is the sample? How close are the sample results (density, basal area) to the real values of the forest? The only way to be 100% sure is to go and measure all the trees in the forest, which is expensive and not practical. The answers lie in the mathematical field of statistics. The math can get complicated but it's necessary and useful.

Calculating a mean (the average number of trees per acre on each plot) is easy. But estimating how well it represents the whole forest (the "population") is a different matter. It depends on variance, which simply means how wide the variation is among the sample plot results. Imagine a completely uniform forest, where all the sample plots give the same number of trees per acre. Then variance is zero: no variation. A single sample plot would be enough. Unfortunately, or rather fortunately, forests aren't like that. Diversity is the name of the game. Let's take the opposite extreme. Imagine a forest so variable that each plot value is far different from the rest. This would result in a high variance: extreme variation. A very large sample would be needed and it still probably would not adequately represent the forest reality.

Two aspects are involved in sampling: the degree of accuracy or precision and probability. The first is how close the sample average is to the real average (the population value) and is expressed in the form of a confidence interval. The second has to do with the likelihood of that result to actually be correct. No sample is a 100% perfect. There is no 100% probability. Foresters usually are happy with a 95% level of probability that their conclusion is correct. 19 times out of 20 (95 out of a 100) it will be right. In the other 1 out of 20 it will not be correct. This is important in planning: making good decisions depends on having reliable information.

Like so many things in life there is an optimum somewhere between two opposing factors. You can spend a lot and have a more precise and probable information to make a decision with less risk or you can spend less and have a less reliable result with higher risk. Spending more means taking a larger sample: more plots and/or bigger plots).

A more challenging matter involving math is forest ecosystem modeling.

Math in forestry: Part 2

The Taos News – Natural Resources Notebook. Sep 3 – 9, 2009. p. B7

Estimating stand density from a sample and ending up with a confidence interval ("there are between 96 and 112 trees per acre and this will be true 95% of the time is just a first step. A more challenging matter is estimating what the outcome will be of a specific action. Which is a more meaningful example of how we use math and statistics in decision making in forest management, whether for preservation or for production.

How will the forest respond if we remove 10% of the trees in thinning? Also, just as important: What if we don't? This involves development and use of predictive models as a planning tool based on math, computer programming and forest science. This is forest ecosystem modeling; it's representing forest stand dynamics through mathematical models. It's a part of systems ecology that involves observing and measuring a phenomenon; formulating, developing, testing, more formulating, further developing and more testing of models.

What is a model? We may think of fashion. We make think of a small airplane that acts like a real full-sized aircraft. Here, we'll think of a complex mathematical model, an equation or a family of equations that are an abstraction of a real system (a forest stand). A lot of the modeling process involves determining what factors affect a certain observable phenomenon. Let's consider tree growth. What factors affect tree growth? What makes a tree grow faster or slower? We can start by listing the most obvious. Genetic make up. What's in its DNA; in its genes? A lot of it's in the species the tree belongs to. Some species like cottonwood or aspen inherently grow faster than other species such as spruce or firs. Just like people, within a species some individuals grow faster and taller than others. Now let's throw in habitat. A tree on a good soil will grow faster than one on a poor soil in a given climatic zone. Another component of habitat is the degree to which other living things are using up habitat resources such as soil nutrients, moisture and solar energy. So competition is a major factor in a tree's growth rate. It is also something that we can manipulate (like through thinning).

Now, how can we put these growth-determining factors into an equation that can be used to predict growth? One answer: through the use of multiple regression analysis. This is a powerful statistical tool that involves math. The results of many observations of tree growth under different conditions can be used to determine which factors are the most important; to put numbers on the magnitude of the relationships and to determine how well they predict variations in the dependent variable. The variable that we are interested in explaining is the dependent variable, that is, it depends (we assume) on the combined effects of determining factors, the independent variables or predicting variables. In our example, tree growth is the dependent variable, which is also called the response variable. Genetic composition, soil, climate and degree of competition are the independent variables that we identify and test. The results of the analysis will tell us which are more important, which are not significant; how closely they can predict growth and finally, what the probability is that our findings are true.

Doing experiments takes time and money. Experimenting using models is faster and more efficient. However they do work together. Models are based on experimentation and serve to integrate results and provide a basis for wider experimentation and support decision-making.

Going from basics, math as we've just finished, back to a factor that is a major concern in planning and modeling, in forest ecosystem behavior, we now adventure into fire.

Managing fire is an important aspect in any kind of forest management. Fire is a natural element. It is major factor in how our forest ecosystems change over time. In recent years there has been a lot of consideration of so-called natural fire regimes; a thing that is difficult to determine and characterize. It requires adequate records over long periods of time, some of which can be gotten from tree ring data and other sources besides direct actual recording.

We usually consider fire a detrimental thing. The Smokey the Bear campaign to create public awareness and help in preventing forest fires, now more commonly referred to as wildfire, is based on the idea that fire is bad. It often is. But it is a natural event that can take place when conditions are right. Fuel build up over time is a major factor. Forests are growing all the time. Trees are constantly growing, dying and being "born" (regenerating in forestry terms). Another obvious factor is climate variation in the form of cycles, where drought is determinant. Interactions with living elements, such as western bark beetle are another important factor.

The following should be an out of the ordinary article series. The idea is to briefly look at fire control and to share the author's personal experience in Alaska in the 1962, 1963 and 1965 fire seasons going into another form of adventure: smokejumping. But first, we'll consider some basic elements of wildfire and related economic and environmental matters.

FIRE AND SMOKEJUMPING

Do we realize the significance of major wildfires on our environment? Consider the temporary loss of a major carbon dioxide sequestering "machine" and add to that the sudden release of carbon into the atmosphere. Fire is one of Nature's tools for renovation, but we have already altered many of Nature's processes, so we shouldn't conform to it, especially when we contribute to the intensity of fire when we suppress smaller fires that Nature starts, thus resulting in an unnatural fuel build up. So the matter of fuel and greenhouse gasses seems like a good way to start this series.

Wildfire: Fuel management and greenhouse gasses

This was the first article published under a new monthly Natural Resources Notebook schedule after taking off for the summer. During my absence New Mexico had its record-breaking fire: The *Las Conchas* Fire in the Jemez mountains.

The Taos News – Natural Resources Notebook. Oct 27 – Nov 2, 2011. p. C2

First of all I'm glad to be back to The Taos News Natural Resources Notebook after taking the summer off. Our readers can look forward to monthly articles appearing the last week of each month. I look forward to readers' comments.

We've had a bad fire season this year here in New Mexico and lately, in Texas. What does it take to make a wildfire? Basically it's fuel, climate/ weather conditions and a spark. Two major considerations: fire occurrence and rate of spread. The first has to do with how a fire starts, the origin of the "spark". The second has to do with how "bad" a fire will be and how difficult to control.

The point here is to consider what factors are susceptible to being managed. What elements can be "controlled". Obviously the climate/ weather factor is not. In our area and the southwest in general we have a dry climate. Northern NM is often referred to as mountain desert. With around 12 to 15 inches of average precipitation, a good part of it in the winter in the form of snow, we are inherently dry. Weather cycles mean that sometimes it less dry and sometimes drier. Day to day, week to week and month to month weather determines the actual fire danger. Temperature, relative humidity and wind and are the main elements that affect how fast a fire will spread for a given fuel situation. Fuel moisture content is an important factor in the equation and is a result of weather and fuel types (light or heavy).

Ignition (the spark) is largely under human control. Most fires are started by people; mostly accidentally, some intentionally. We are all familiar with public awareness and education in preventing wildfire. However history has shown that there will always be "sparks". Natural ignition is from lightning, which is a major cause of forest fires. The combination climate/weather, fuel increase through forest growth and lightning-caused fire is a part of natural forest ecosystem dynamics.

So here we'll concentrate on fuel being the element that we can have the most control over. Gradual increase in fuel is taking place constantly in forest ecosystems through growth and mortality. Growth increases the living above ground fuel in the form of tree crowns, branches, leaves and tree trunks. Mortality provides the dead dry fuel in the form of leaves (including pine-needles) branches, standing and downed tree trunks. Regeneration (new trees being born) in the replacement of mortality and provides the basis for new growth.

Consider the term fuel management in reducing losses to wildfire. We can reduce living fuel through removal of live trees in thinning and timber harvesting. Dead dry fuel can be removed by physically gathering it, by prescribed burning or both.

Through fuel management, the intensity and rate of spread can be affected, partially controlled, within the limits of un-controllable weather conditions. The more fuel, the hotter the fire and greater the rate of spread will be under a given set of weather conditions. Another thing to consider: The more fuel, the greater the amount of Carbon that will be released into the atmosphere. How much Carbon (in the form of carbon dioxide - CO_2) was put into the atmosphere in the Las Conchas fire? Consider the ratio of tons of Carbon to tons of fuel. How much less Carbon would have been released if more of the forest had been treated through thinning, timber harvesting (including fire-wood

 FOREST POWER Adventures in Ecology and Forest Management

cutting) and prescribed burning? Here we have a major benefit of costly fuel reduction efforts.

Is fire always bad? Is wildfire or forest fire good or bad? For whom or for what?

We have made the connection between fire intensity, the environment and forest management practices. Now we'll add an important element in the over all sustainability of dealing with forests: jobs. This is both an economic and a political aspect of sustainability.

Wildfire: Forest fuel management and Jobs

The Taos News – Natural Resources Notebook. Nov 23 - 30, 2011. p. B 13

Fuel management in forest ecosystems to improve forest health and reduce loss to fire is labor intensive. Sustainable forest treatment involves a wide range of activities in planning, field preparation, the actual treatment and follow up monitoring of the ecosystems' responses to treatment. It is an economically and environmentally sustainable jobs program that needs to be considered.

Fuel management involves reducing living fuel (removing live trees) in timber harvesting and thinning and handling dead fuel, usually and most economically, by prescribed burning. Wood gathering and, in some instances, chipping are other means of fuel reduction.

For many, what comes to mind might be that we are suggesting that forests be sacrificed to provide jobs. This is definitely not the case. There is no sacrifice, only improvement. What we are pointing out is that we can have a "win – win +" situation. We win on the side of the environment by having healthier forests with less fire spread (less total burn area), less Carbon dioxide greenhouse gas (CO2) released into the atmosphere when fires occur on treated areas (less fuel, less Carbon) and more CO2 taken from the atmosphere through enhanced growth. Growth is maximized in forest stands kept at normal stocking (not too thick, not too sparse).

We win on the side of sustainable jobs. We also win on the side of enhanced education and training, revenue generation and green forest products, as well as other environmental services, such as cleaner air, enhanced water production on treated watersheds and enhanced wildlife habitat through spatial and biological diversity as a result of forest treatment.

"Sustainable jobs" means that forest treatment is continuous, taking on successive areas on a rotation basis, while ensuring ecosystem sustainability in that only net growth is removed in successive timber harvest and thinning operations under a sustainable cutting cycle. It also means that most, if not all, of the treatment will be paid for by the products removed, meaning economic and fiscal sustainability provided that we can achieve a modern forest industry.

This is a "win-win-win" situation if we are willing to consider it and try it out on selected pilot areas that can be closely monitored by all concerned parties.

How many sustainable jobs can be created? What kinds of jobs? Who creates them? First of all, taking the questions in reverse, both the public and private sectors on public and private forests. Planning and preparation would be done under the close supervision of public entities, federal and state forestry, but many specific tasks can be contracted out to private operators. The latter would be mostly small businesses specialized in the diverse tasks going from mapping to marking trees or areas for removal. The actual treatment would be undertaken by private business, again mostly small to medium. An example of a small family business would be in cutting and removal of small dimension material. Larger trees require more specialized equipment and personnel, but are the source of the major part of economic sustainability of the operations. Many high-tech jobs in geographic information systems (GIS) modeling, remote sensing (using satellite images) and field global positioning system (GPS) mapping would be created and the corresponding student science, technology, engineering and math (STEM) careers enhanced.

Fuel management is only for suitable forests, meaning topography, soils, stand conditions and accessibility. This has the effect of ensuring a balance between treated and untreated areas of forest.

And now on to the adventures of smokejumping.

Smokejumping in Alaska

The Taos News – Natural Resources Notebook. July 1 – 7, 2010. p. B5

2010 marks 70 years of smokejumping in the US. Parachuting as a quick means of getting firefighters on a fire actually started in Russia in the

1930's. The National Smokejumper Association (NSA) 2010 reunion took place in Redding, CA one of several jump bases. The Forest Service Missoula base is the biggest and most well known. Fairbanks, Alaska is a BLM jumper base.

Smokejumpers are identified by their jumper base and rookie training year. Mine is FBX-62 (Fairbanks, Alaska, 1962). At the Redding reunion active and retired jumpers got together to share experiences and see what members are doing; also to remember ones who are no longer with us. Group pictures were taken by jumper base. It was great to catch up with old companions.

Our Fairbanks 1962 group was made up of Fire Control Aides (FCA's) that were invited to train as jumpers. Originally FCA's were trained in fire behavior, initial attack strategies and techniques, equipment operation (pumps and chainsaws) and administrative tasks aimed at getting temporary fire fighters paid. We were to go in after the jumpers when they weren't able to put out a fire on initial attack when it becomes a project fire. The base officials apparently decided that there was no reason why the FCA's couldn't jump along with the regular jumpers, so we did. The regular jumpers referred to us as gyppo-jumpers, meaning that they felt that we weren't the real thing. The term "gyppo" comes from sort of temporary logging outfits, often salvage operators that are called "gyppo loggers".

Smokejumping in Alaska is much softer than in the lower 48. We did not have to worry much about landing on rocks or hanging up in a tree over 50 feet tall. Training involves learning to do Allen Rolls on landing. In Alaska we seldom had to do them since landing on the tundra was like a feather bed compared to the Missoula, Redding, Cave Junction, Silver City and other base jumping.

In at least one major fire, three FCA's were left in charge after the rest of the 13-man crew was pulled out and Eskimo crews ferried in by helicopter. This took place after the fire over-ran the heliport that we had prepared making an opening and putting down a pad of logs to allow the choppers to land on the soft tundra.

The "Doug 3" (DC3) carries a 13-person (there are women jumpers) jumper crew with equipment. Once over the fire, the spotter guides the pilot and uses streamers to test the wind and determine where to let the jumpers out in order to land in a designated spot, hopefully not in the fire. Jumpers leave the plane in 3-man sticks. The first and second make orderly exits from the door while the third sort of stumbles out. The signal to jump is a whack on the back of the leg that lets you know in no uncertain terms that it's time to step out.

We used small black spruce tops as beaters. Building fire line is slow and involves clearing mostly black spruce and using a pulaski to dig a trench through the tundra down to permafrost. This had to be repeatedly done to remove dry duff left as the permafrost melts.

As far as I know Taos has two smokejumpers: the other one is John (Jock) L. Fleming (Missoula-49), a fellow Colorado State University forestry graduate.

Smokejumping in Alaska: Part 2

The Taos News – Natural Resources Notebook. July 15 - 21, 2010. p. B10

As we sat around the campfire at "night" (no darkness, no headlamps) the Eskimo crew taught me a few words. The one I remember most was "goofac" (spelling?): coffee. I was told it came from the Alaska's previous owners, the Russians (remember Seward's folly?); from notes in my memory the phrase goofac ky-yewghktoe (sorry it's my own phonetics) meant I want some coffee or do you want coffee. So much for my memory notes. The crew was great sharing experiences on living near the Arctic Circle in western Alaska.

Our 13-man initial attack crew jumped from the DC3. We were not able to make much headway on the fire, which was out of control. We had to move our landing site temporary base and gear and lost our first helipad to it. Finally ground crews were ferried in by military chopper and all but three of the jumpers ferried out to go on to other fires started in the lightning bust, patrolled by the P51 Mustang WWII fighter plane that the BLM pilots fought over (not literally) to fly. Three of us FCA's were left to manage the fire. It took several days and some rain to get it under control and put out. We had a Bell G3 helicopter to see the fire from a birds-eye perspective and plan strategies. From quite a distance away the heat from the head of the fire could be felt in the chopper (flown without doors so one could lean out). Smokejumping in Alaska is an essential tool in fire control given the distances and lack of roads. It's common to fly for over two or three hours in the DC3 or the Grumman Goose (amphibian twin-engine that carries four jumpers) to get to a fire. Leading up to such a fire experience, training is a critical element in smokejumping.

Rookie (first-time training - 1962) involved jumping from the shock tower, which simulates jumping and the parachute opening shock. It teaches one how to try to keep a good position during the brief freefall until the chute is opened by the static line attached to the plane. Let-downs teach one how to get down from a tree in the rare event in Alaska when the jumper hangs up. My highest let-down on a fire was all of three feet. Learning the Allen Rolls was the most difficult for me (other than that first time off the shock tower - worse than the first training jump). Our jump instructors, Gene DeBruin and Gid Newton helped me after hours. They both went on to work as cargo droppers in Southeast Asia and unfortunately didn't come back. Other training involved rope and tree climbing, jogging and lots of other exercises. The final training event was the series of seven practice jumps. The first was from the Goose with one man jumping at a time. The Goose has a small jump door with handles overhead that allow you to swing out. In that first jump the land below at 1000 feet above the ground looked like a picture there being no real sense of height. With the wind rushing through the facemask mesh waiting for the whack on the back of leg from the spotter, time seems to stand still. There is a brief warning when the spotter tells the pilot to throttle down to reduce prop wash during exit. Training on the shock tower also teaches one to check the chute's canopy right after the opening shock. Look for a line crossed over the canopy which increases the rate of fall. This can be fixed by cutting the line with the hunting knife attached to the reserve chute. The worst case is a streamer where the chute streams out of the packing but fails to open. The reserve chute must be used. An intermediate situation is where several lines cross over the canopy dividing it into two parts like a brassiere. It's called a Mae West. Malfunctions fortunately are rare. I never had one out of a total of 33 jumps, 20 practice and 13 fire. All in all smokejumping has a good safety record. The greatest loss was in Mann Gulch where eleven jumpers perished in the fire.

Smokejumping in Alaska: Part 3

The Taos News – Natural Resources Notebook. July 29 – Aug 4, 2010. p. B8

What does a typical fire jump in Alaska look like? It starts with a call over the Fairbanks jumper base PA system for the first jumpers on the rotating list. Usually depending on the fire danger, the top 13 jumpers on the list (a Doug-load–DC3) are kept nearby the base loading platform, their gear assembled and ready to go. This time the call is for the first four to load up and head for the airport. This is a

Goose-load. The BLM amphibious Grumman Goose carries four jumpers, the spotter and equipment. The jumpers suit up on the tarmac and take off in the Goose.

Their destination, two small fires started by lightning reported by commercial pilots on their routine routes. The flight takes around an hour and a quarter with the jump door open (though it can be opened in flight). As the plane approaches the first fire, the jumpers tighten their harnesses and again check each others' main chutes and static lines. The spotter guides the pilot in a circle over the fire and chooses a landing spot dropping streamers, weighted paper objects that simulate the time it takes from jump to landing, usually at an altitude of 1000 feet above the ground. This allows the spotter to decide where to drop the jumpers so that they have the best chance of landing near the target. When he's satisfied it's time to go. The two jumpers are at the door, the second is crouched behind the first. It's a two-man stick, meaning two jumpers go one right after the other. After a brief instruction to the pilot to cut throttle (to reduce prop wash, the air blast that hits the jumper on exit), the spotter whacks the back of the leg of the first jumper and he swings out using the handles over the door. The second jumper follows with the delay needed to keep them apart.

Once the chute is opened by the static line and the canopy checked to make sure it's OK, the jumpers guide themselves toward the landing spot. The old round 32-foot chutes had slots that are closed by pulling the marked lines. Closing a slot on the right side makes the chute turn right, sort of like using the individual brakes on a tractor to help turn. On landing the second thing to do, once untangled from the collapsed chute, is to break out the mosquito repellent; then radio the pilot and spotter that all is well and to prepare for the cargo drop of equipment and C-rations, the latter dumped out of the plane without chutes, the tundra cushioning their fall. Equipment includes a Pulaski, sleeping bag extra repellent but no headlamp needed during fire season. It never gets dark; the sun only dips under the horizon just before midnight to return just after.

Mosquitoes on the tundra are one's worst enemies; they're much more than an inconvenience. Although in contrast to the tropics where there are some (but nothing compares to tundra where they have no frogs or other enemies), there's no danger of disease but people have been known to go crazy under the constant onslaught of clouds of the little buggers. In fact, one of the causes of fires is the need to have a smoke screen to ward them off. Prospectors and placer miners frequently used fire for this purpose not having the benefit of repellents.

Usually this kind of two-manner is out in a few hours. Then the jumpers must stay on to make sure it's completely out checking with hands feeling for the warmth of remaining embers, In tundra this usually is no problem since it acts like grassfire with little or no heavy fuel.

You're out in the middle of nowhere with only your buddy. You only have radio contact when one of the BLM planes is overhead. It's kind of an uneasy feeling. Then it's all over and time to pack out to the nearest lake or river to be picked up by the Goose. Hiking in the tundra is a bear and progress slow, especially with all the gear.

A thought: Should we really have been putting out naturally caused fires?

Smokejumping in Alaska: Part 4

The Taos News – Natural Resources Notebook. Aug 25 – Sep 1, 2010. p. B12

Fire control in Alaska was not only work. Having my 51-Chevy made it possible to get out on weekends when we were not on standby. One great outing was a weekend trip to Valdez, the beautiful town with so friendly people. This was sometime in May or early June, 1963. Tragically the town and many people were lost in the 1964 earthquake. I have been told that the town was rebuilt on higher ground. Having a car in Fairbanks was quite a luxury for our fire control workers, both smokejumpers and others. It meant being able to explore the old gold dredges and pan for gold. We actually got enough to be able to see it in a tiny jar. We also explored glaciers and even met up with a grizzly bear, fortunately at a good distance. It ran away before we headed in the opposite direction. We did see wolves from the air. At that time there was still a $50 bounty on them.

Having the car meant having the great experience of driving to Fairbanks. Going from San Cristobal, just north of Taos, to Fairbanks was quite an adventure in itself. Travel to Calgary, Canada on paved highways with frequent gas stations and services was pretty routine, but the Alcan highway was something else: 1500 miles of gravel on the way back in late August after the fire season had ended; snow packed on the way up in late march, very much still winter. I got stuck in a snowdrift north of Whitehorse and was rescued by a truck driver. All drivers are especially considerate on the Alcan, always stopping to ask if I needed help even though I was taking a picture. The average distance between roadhouses (gas and food) was around 60 miles. It took eight days for the 4000 some miles, including the frequent stops to sleep in the car and enjoy the scenery.

The car also was a headache for our jump-base managers. They didn't appreciate our not staying around the base on weekends. We didn't appreciate not being paid for standby. The last straw was when Phil Clark (Cave Junction) had to buzz us from a plane while we were at work panning gold. I remember him sticking his head out calling for us to get back to the base for a fire call. That got us sent to McGrath effectively separating us from my wheels. The McGrath experience was great. We enjoyed station work, mostly maintenance, during lulls in fire activity. Other great stations were Fort Yukon (not far from Dawson, Yukon Territory, Canada) and Delta Junction (Tanana).

I did get to one fire on the coast near Deering on the tip of the Seward Peninsula. This one was not a jump but a drive and walk in. I was dropped off at the airport and hired transportation to the fire. Just after the fire was pretty much out, we were hit with 24 hours of steady rain. The hired jeep was under water and we had to hike back over 20 miles. A placer miner near the site of the fire pulled the jeep out of the swollen river with his tundra cat (tracked vehicle). This was open tundra without a tree in sight anywhere.

Boreal forests in Alaska are mostly sparse thin crowned black spruce (Picea mariana) over wide areas and the larger white spruce (Picea glauca) along the rivers with a few broadleaf trees, mostly birch and alder. Undergrowth is mostly tundra with blueberry and other shrubs. The wide, mostly flat, expanses with meandering rivers probably are a floodplain type of landscape. Tundra, whether under forest or in the open, is a thick insulating "blanket" that maintains the permafrost, which is a relic left over from the last ice age. Once the tundra is removed by fire or other alteration, permafrost does not come back. This was part of reasoning behind fire control. Tundra vegetation takes over 100 years to regenerate (minus the permafrost). The areas described here are interior Alaska, which is completely different from the coast and from southeast Alaska with its more temperate rich forests and biodiversity.

Rowena Gibson kindly told me about two other local BLM Alaska smokejumpers, Rene and Dalan Romero of Taos Pueblo.

Now let's venture south to Bolivia and Venezuela for a taste of tropical forest ecology and management. It's a different "ballgame" both ecologically and socially. However, many of the same principles and problems encountered in our temperate forests, and many more challenges and adventures are involved in understanding and dealing with tropical forest ecosystems and their human environment with all its social, economic and political complexities.

TROPICAL HUMID FOREST (THF) MANAGEMENT

What are tropical rainforests?

The Taos News – Natural Resources Notebook. May 6 - 12, 2010. p. B7

What are tropical rainforests?

The term is widely used referring to tropical forests, but is it really a rainforest? True rainforests are characterized by very high average annual precipitation, on the order of 157 to 236 inches (4000 to 6000 mm), although when you look up "rainforest" you find that precipitation above 50 inches (1270 mm) is considered rainforest. Actually very few tropical forests fall under the extreme definition of this category. For example, in the Amazon-Orinoco basins in South America, tropical forests for the most part are closer to around 80 to 120 annual rainfall (1800 to 2500 mm). A better term for these forests is humid tropical forest (or tropical humid forest).

When referring to the most common types of tropical forests we can use the term humid tropical forest and reserve rainforest for the more extreme conditions. The term tropical high forest (THF) is also used to refer to both general forest types. This is in contrast to dry tropical forest or tropical dry forest generally with annual precipitation under 47 inches (1200 mm) concentrated in a relatively short rainy season. Tropical dry forests usually don't have a continuous canopy but have relatively isolated trees less than around 60 feet tall standing out over a thick, spiny lower level of trees under around 30 feet height.

There are true tropical rainforests along the west coast of Colombia around Buenaventura (Bajo Calima) with annual rainfall up to 236 inches (6000 mm). This is comparable to our temperate rainforests on the Olympic Peninsula in Washington State.

Some humid tropical forests are markedly seasonal, characterized by a well-defined dry season. Deciduous or semi-deciduous forests are common in seasonal tropical forest types. For example the High Western Llano forests of Venezuela, in the eastern piedmont of the Andes in the state of Barinas, have an annual precipitation around 47 to 70 inches (1200 to 1800 mm) and a three to four-month dry season with practically no precipitation. These forests would be classified as seasonal sub-humid tropical forests (borderline humid tropical forest) and fall under the category of tropical high forest in that they have a well-developed but not too dense canopy at around 65 to 80 feet height (20 to 25 m) with emerging trees up to or above 115 feet (35 m). Trees that are typical of the latter are the now almost extinct mahogany (Swietenia macrophyla), cigar-box cedar (Cedrela odorata) and saqui-saqui (Bombacopsis quinata). The Caparo forest area in the state of Barinas, Venezuela, is an example of seasonal tropical forest. Most of the Caparo Forest Reserve has been lost to squatting and conversion to cattle ranching. Only a 7,000-hectare area remains that is managed by the Universidad de Los Andes (Merida) as a biological reserve and is under constant squatting pressure.

Soils play a major role in determining the characteristics of a tropical forest. The Caparo seasonal forests are on an alluvial floodplain landscape, where soil drainage is a critical habitat factor. On the heavy clay soils we find deciduous forests (or in extreme cases, no forest at all), whereas on well-drained soils we find broadleaf evergreen forests (not conifers). We also find deciduous forests on excessively drained sandy soils formed along the banks of the ever-migrating rivers. So within a given climatic region, forest types vary greatly with soil.

In many tropical regions widespread poverty and weak governmental institutions are responsible for the loss of tropical forests.

Forest management in Bolivia's subtropical seasonal forest

The Taos News – Natural Resources Notebook. Feb 21 - 27, 2008

What is a sub-tropical seasonal forest?

Most of Bolivia's forests are located in the eastern lowlands region, much of which belongs to the Amazon basin. My experience in Bolivia is limited to the sub-tropical forests of the Beni, near San Borja and San Ignacio de Moxos (just under 15 degrees south latitude) which are located mostly on an alluvial floodplain terrain, where other than climate, soil drainage is the main factor of the forest habitat. The general character of the forest is that of a tropical forest with a fairly even mean temperature of around

25 degrees C and 1800 mm annual precipitation, most of which occurs during the four or five-month rainy season, roughly from December to April, hence the term "seasonal". The mean monthly temperature during the southern hemisphere "winter" which coincides with the dry season, is slightly lowered by the effect of the "surazos" which are masses of cool air that move northward from the Antarctic. Due to poor soil drainage, the forest is not as dense as a typical humid tropical forest. The Beni sub-tropical type of forest was rich in mahogany ("mara" or "caoba"). "Was" refers to its near depletion due to the spotty nature of occurrence of this species, its high value, it's lack of reproduction (regeneration) in unaltered forest conditions and the impossibility of effective timber harvest control due to difficult accessibility (difficult for forestry personnel but not for "timber poachers" who use chainsaws to saw the logs into squared timbers or thick boards transportable by hand and dugout canoe).

My consulting work was on the Chimanes forest management project for the Bolivian Government and the International Tropical Timber Organization (ITTO) whose objective is for all timber traded on the world market to come from certified sustainable management. A large area of the native forest lands has been assigned (returned) to the Tsimane (Chimán) Native-American people for their use. The Tsimane are a forest people whose traditional livelihood comes mostly from harvesting forest products, notably jatata palm woven roofing panels, wild honey, poles for light construction and firewood for income as well as various foods, medicines and fibre for subsistence, including small "slash and burn" farm plots (chaques). Now they have timber sale income from a 40,000 acre sustainable management unit near San Borja.

Forest management plans have been in effect under a long-term concession regime to timber companies in other areas of the Chimanes Forest. The management units vary from 50,000 ha to 100,000 ha (approximately 124,000 to 247,000 acres) under 20-year contracts with the Bolivian government. Such delegated management is meant to be sustainable, however there were severe limitations that were detrimental to sustainability which included the extreme selectivity of the timber harvest, lack of roads, and to a certain extent lack of authority on the part of forestry officials in making sure that management guidelines were followed and inability to prevent widespread "timber poaching". Selectivity refers to the fact that most of the standing timber value was in a single species, mahogany. This made it extremely difficult to spread out timber harvest over a long enough period of time to allow some form of regeneration. The spotty nature of occurrence of mahogany trees further complicates the situation. What we usually do in tropical forestry is define annual cutting areas in order to regulate timber harvest spatially and in time. Logging must be completed in a unit before authorization is issued to start the next. "Completed logging" in a tropical or sub-tropical forest means that all designated trees of commercial species are removed. Since these usually make up less that 5% of the total number of trees per unit area in the forest, only a very small proportion of the forest is actually removed. Typically a hectare, 2.47 acres, will have around 300 trees counting all those above four inches in diameter, typically belonging to over 75 species. Only around three or four trees are removed in logging. An additional number of trees are damaged in the logging process. The number of such units is set so that there is a period of time long enough to allow regeneration of the commercial species before the same area is subjected to a new harvest. This is the cutting cycle and by law in Bolivia cannot be less than 20 years. We usually recommend a cycle of 30 or more years to cover uncertainties in natural forest regeneration or regeneration by planting.

At present sustainability will more likely be achieved under better market conditions (not depending solely on mahogany) in the Chimanes Forest. In most tropical and sub-tropical forests, a fair degree of sustainability can be achieved simply through adequate timber harvest regulation which requires an efficient administration and political willingness. There is great need of multi-party monitoring in order to effectively evaluate management and to enhance credibility. The main threat to sustainability is of political and socio-economic nature related to uncontrolled conversion of the forest to agriculture (squatting).

Again, special thanks to Debbie Ragland, UNM-Taos Geology, for her valuable contribution in reviewing and editing.

Tropical seasonal forests in Venezuela

The Taos News – Natural Resources Notebook. May 20 - 26, 2010. p. B14

What are tropical seasonal forests and what is happening to them in Venezuela?

A band of humid and sub-humid tropical forest used to exist in Venezuela between the Andes and the grasslands to the east. The area is a piedmont alluvial floodplain under 500 feet elevation, obviously in Earth's tropical zone. It is flat with only minute relief, usually less than around ten feet in variation from the low bajios to the high bancos. Annual rainfall varies from 47 to 70 inches (1200 to 1800 mm). Mean annual temperature is around 78 degrees F (25.6 degrees C). The greatest variations occur from early morning with the cool breeze coming off the Andes, to early afternoon, when it can reach the upper nineties. There is a well-defined four-month dry season from mid-December to mid-April, during which there is practically no precipitation. As a result, the seasonal tropical forest's growing season is limited by precipitation (availability of water in the ecosystems) in contrast to our climate where it's the availability of heat (frost-free months).

These forests can be considered sub-humid tropical forests (borderline humid tropical forest) and fall under the category of tropical high forest in that they have a well-developed canopy at around 65 to 80 feet tall (20 to 25 m) with emerging trees up to or above 115 feet (35 m), such as mahogany and cigar-box cedar. The alluvial floodplain landscape determines that soil drainage is a critical habitat factor. Soil parental material is still being laid down as sediments (sands, clays and silts) carried by the rivers that often change course, meaning that the soils are young and relatively fertile.

Tree species composition is quite complex in tropical forests in general. In our seasonal tropical forests, despite a shorter growing season (as compared to humid tropical forests) and soil drainage limitations, on an average hectare (2.47 acres) we find 70 or more tree species. Stand densities (trees/hectare) are over 300 trees. The larger trees can have diameters of over six feet. Palm trees are abundant. As in tropical forests in general, typically only a few species are of commercial value and often only amount to less than 10 individuals per hectare (4/acre). This depends greatly on market conditions, economics of management and harvesting (logging) and wood product technology.

During the 1940's and 50's mahogany and cigar-box cedar were logged under an annual permit regime in which the only obligation was to implement minimum diameter cutting specifications and re-planting at the rate of five trees for every tree harvested. Later, in the early 1960's, long-term forest management concessions were established. Timber companies were authorized to harvest timber on pre-designated annual compartments and were in charge of silviculture (mainly tree planting), protection, road building and maintenance under sustainable management plans approved and supervised by the national government forest authorities.

Now, why the past tense?

Even though large areas of these forests were designated national forest reserves and most of them under sustainable management, encroachment by squatters and conversion to agriculture took a heavy toll on them. By the year 2000 all but the Caparo 7000-hectare biological reserve managed by the Universidad de Los Andes had been deforested and converted to agriculture. Even now this bio-reserve is under constant squatting pressure. A combination of impoverished rural populations, weak governmental institutions and outright political manipulation is responsible for the loss of these forests.

Tropical seasonal forests in Venezuela: Part 2

The Taos News – Natural Resources Notebook. June 3 - 9, 2010. p. B5

Tropical forests, and for that matter all forests, are immersed in a social and political environment which must be taken into account, no matter what society decides to do with that resource. This is especially true for the tropics with its effect on forest management whether for preservation or production. So, we will begin to consider these factors in the present series of articles on tropical forests while sharing experiences from living in Venezuela from 1966 to 2004.

During the early 1960's four national forest reserves (reservas forestales) were established in the tropical seasonal forest; the belt described in the previous article, which is part of the western high llanos of Venezuela. The idea was to conserve, under sustainable productive management, portions of the once extensive forests in the belt. Prior to the early 1960's, these forests had been "high-graded" with logging of mahogany and cigar-box cedar under an annual permits and minimum cutting diameters regime. It is to be noted that even relatively un-regulated logging in a tropical forest does not have the impact that one would imagine. This is because only a very few trees species are of commercial value, which means that often less than 10 trees per hectare (4/acre) out of over 300 trees per hectare (120/acre) are harvested. The forest reserve figure was established primarily for sustainable timber production. This takes place within a political setting.

The following text was deleted in publication, but is included here in order to present a better picture of how forest management is related to politics and ideology, especially in Venezuela.

Venezuela emerged from its last dictatorship, that of Marco Perez Jimenez, in 1958. The Direccion General de Recursos Naturales Renovables under the Ministry of Agriculture (MAC: Ministerio de Agricultura y Cria) was in charge of the administration of the newly established forest reserves under the first post-Perez Jimenez democratic president, Romulo Betancourt of the Accion Democratica (AD) political party. This was a left-center administration that for some wasn't far enough to the left, resulting in the Movimiento de Izquierda Revolucionaria (MIR) splitting off in 1960, which, along with the Partido Comunista de Venezuela (PCV), were involved in a guerilla movement.

This is relevant in that during the early sixties, coming out of a situation of guerilla warfare, it was not easy for a forester to work in the field.

In 1966 at one point I was thoroughly checked at a special forces (*Cazadores*) military road checkpoint (*alcabala*). The problem was that I had a compass and other forestry field gear and some books with underlined items (I was still a student). After much questioning I was allowed to continue on my way after the official, in a friendly way, asked if I knew how to play the cuatro (Venezuelan 4-stringed musical instrument) that I also had with me. The porpuesto driver was quite relieved as we continued on our way on the highway between Guanare and Barinas.

Social problems and rural poverty fueled pressure on seasonal tropical forests that were rapidly being converted to agriculture. By the mid 1960's one of the forest reserves had completely succumbed to illegal (squatting) conversion even before organized forest management could get started. The once rich in mahogany and cigar box cedar Turen Forest Reserve, near Acarigua in the state of Portuguesa, unfortunately (for the forest) was located on fairly rich alluvial soils in easily accessible terrain. The result was rapid conversion to a breadbasket type of agriculture with crops in sesame (ajonjolí), corn and sorghum. Only a small experimental area survived there for a time.

The loss of tropical forests is a major concern for environmentalists and for everybody who lives and breathes. The matter involves complex social and political aspects, poverty being at the root of them.

Tropical seasonal forests in Venezuela: Part 3

The Taos News – Natural Resources Notebook. June 17 - 23, 2010. p. B12

How was the tropical seasonal forest (TSF) lost?

The process of "colonization" meaning occupying forest areas begins with the need for farming and ranching lands. A large area of unoccupied forest is an open invitation to put it to human use as we did in the early stage of our colonization en the northeast. The main traditional use of land is to produce food. Before highways were built in the TSF belt on the eastern side of the Andes, there were only sporadic areas mostly by people going down into the lowlands from the land-scarce valleys of the Andes. Colonists (conuqueros) had to deal with many adverse factors, among them malaria, lack of means of transportation, schools and medical facilities. Once the main highway was built between Barinas and San Cristobal, colonization and conversion of forestlands proceeded rapidly. The designation of the Ticoporo Forest Reserve in the early 1960's was an attempt to conserve at least a part of the forest. Towns along the highway grew rapidly as people were attracted to the area in a sort of spontaneous homesteading process. Public lands, including the forests, called baldíos, were open to occupation. Human needs, poverty and the political pressure of large numbers of people put the survival of the forest reserve under huge strain.

The 270,000-hectare Ticoporo Forest Reserve had four units: I, II, III and an Experimental Unit. Long-term management concessions were set up with different modes of investment. Unit I was to be managed by a coop of farmers and was called Empresa Campesina; Unit II by a totally private enterprise managed by the sawmill and plywood business CONTACA. Unit III was managed by EMALLCA, which was a partnership company of private business and public sector, the University of the Andes (ULA). The Experimental Unit was totally under public administration.

To make a long story short, there was an inverse relationship between the degree of private development and loss of the forest to agriculture by squatting; the greater the proportion of public sector involvement, the faster and more intense the loss to squatting. By the 1970's, Unit I had been almost completely converted to agriculture, mostly cattle ranching. By the early 1980's more than half of the Experimental Unit had been occupied and converted and by mid 80's only a small area under

---

    FOREST POWER Adventures in Ecology and Forest Management

administration of the ULA was left, mostly in plantations of teak and melina (exotic species). Unit II was the last to succumb to conversion around the year 2000 when the concession was cancelled by the Chavez administration. Today there is practically no forest left in Ticoporo.

The deforestation conversion process takes place as follows: First, small family conucos are established by rural peasants (campesinos) that move into an area, progressively cutting down the forest using fire (slash and burn). They grow corn as a cash crop and plantain, yuca (cassava root) and raise animals for subsistence. After 2 to 3 years the soil is worn out. The small squatters who have done the hard work of deforestation sell their small temporary farms to cattle ranchers, usually small operators who consolidate their ranches into larger holdings by buying other ranches. This results in a process of converting what used to be forest into medium to large cattle ranches. The soils, though depleted for corn, sustain grass for cattle.

The struggle between human needs and conservation is evident in loss of tropical forests.

Having completed our discussion on ecology and forest management matters and our brief tour south into the tropics and sub-tropics of Venezuela and Bolivia, we'll cap our adventure going into a final discussion on our approach to the environment and some thoughts on the role of corporations.

DEALING WITH OUR ENVIRONMENT

Our environment: Protect it or manage it?

The Taos News – Natural Resources Notebook. Feb 7 - 13, 2008. P. B11

We use the term "environmental protection" or the phrase "protect our environment" but is it too late for that? Would it be better to state that we need to manage it?

Is it too late to protect our environment? We protect something that is in good shape and which we want to keep that way. "Good" (or we could use a better term: "good enough") means that we are satisfied with it, which implies that it meets our objectives, both present and future. If that something (our environment) is not in "good" or "good enough" shape, then we would want to improve it rather than protect it. How would we evaluate the state of our environment at present? If it's good enough, then we are correct in using the term environmental protection; if not then "environmental management" would be a more appropriate term. Environmental management involves applying knowledge obtained from environmental science to specific manageable aspects in order to produce results that improve our environment. It combines science with technology (which involves the "how to do it" aspects of management); economics which involves the "with what resources" to do it and optimization in the allocation of resources (mainly money); managerial science which involves the administration of organizations and projects in achieving goals, including personnel management, information technology (data processing, simulation models, optimization models, statistical analyses and all disciplines that constitute operations research technology); and politics which involves the determination of who decides in governing and general over-seeing, under what set of rules and regulations (legislation), how laws are applied and the consequences of not following the laws (the judicial aspect). We could consider philosophical aspects such as for whom or for what we want to manage our environment. Is it for the human species? Or is it for the good of all life, or even the planet Earth as a whole. I assume that we are egocentric and that we are most interested in our own survival and that that means also the wellbeing for the earth ecosystem (our house) as a whole. There is a technical journal titled, "Environmental Management" published by Springer, New York ISSN 0364-152X (print) 1432-1009 (online). Its subject scope is specified as "Business and Economics, Earth and Environmental Science, Nature Conservation , Environmental Management , Forest Management, Ecology, Environment, Atmospheric Protection/Air Quality Control/Air Pollution and Waste Water Technology / Water Pollution Control / Water Management / Aquatic Pollution" (information from SpringerLink from http://www.springerlink.com/content/100370/). A case in point on our atmosphere and climate change: Protection would seem to mean that we try to reduce our greenhouse gas emissions while management would mean that we do that but also try to remove greenhouses gasses by proactive means.

Before we go on, it would be a good idea to define the term "environment". We often use a term so much that we sort of take it for granted and even lose perspective of its full meaning. As I pointed out in a previous article, ecology is the study (logies, hence ology) of our "house" (oikos) and our relation with it. Our environment is the total of everything that we live in. It's our big "house". It would help to specify different aspects as examples of elements of the environment which include the atmosphere (related to pollution and climate change); water, which includes fresh water bodies (rivers, streams and lakes) and oceans; soils (which include mineral and biological components); and biological elements (biodiversity) which include plants (forests, grasslands, tundra, etc.) and other animals (besides us), all of which are part of our environment. It would seem that all this is obvious but it would pay for us to think in depth on these and others aspects.

As we can appreciate, environmental management is a wide field that encompasses most everything. What we are trying to get across is the idea of managing our environment, the scope of the subject and its importance and the holistic nature of the whole idea. It does seem that it is too late for protection, meaning we need to improve our environment and that we should consider or adopt the term environmental management which means that we recognize this state of affairs and are willing to do something about it. Should we change the "EPA" to "EMA"? We probably won't want to go that far, at least for now!

Environmental activism is a serious, complex matter. Under the precautionary principle we tend to say no and ask questions later. This may be an understandable approach, but it also can cause more harm than good. A more reasonable approach is to go into depth and consider all possible consequences of a proposed action. This requires expertise and is time and resource consuming. However, the resources will be well invested in view of the profound nature of most environmental decisions. Credibility is a major factor in trust on the part of the general public in our authorities. And we must keep in mind that economic and socio-political sustainability must go hand in hand with environmental sustainability.

Environmental decisions: Just say no or consider

The Taos News – Natural Resources Notebook. Feb 23 – 29, 2012. p. C2

When there is an environmental concern over a proposed project, it would seem that the approach often taken is to "just say no". Is "stop the Keystone Pipeline" or stop a timber sale on a national forest the best way to go about addressing the matter? There is an alternative approach based on "let's look at it in detail and decide if it can be done safely for the environment before just trying to block it.

Rationality is necessary to have a balanced approach to solving decision-making problems. The decision: to do or not to do. Either way there are consequences, both those that are intended (desired) or those that are unintended (collateral damage?). The latter often can do more harm than good, meaning the detrimental outcomes outweigh the benefits.

First, a case in point: The Keystone Pipeline project is a major undertaking that has a wide range of impacts and consequences. On the proponents' side: energy independence, jobs and, yes even environmental benefits (oil through a pipeline may be safer than transported over oceans). On the opponents' side: environmental danger to vital aquifers. First of all let's consider the opponents' agenda's both stated and possibly "hidden" agenda. Danger of aquifer pollution is obviously a valid concern. But before "saying no" shouldn't we be asking if it can be done safely with a degree of certainty comparable to other endeavors? Can the pipeline be built in such a way as to minimize the danger? We must realize that nothing is 100% sure. We must balance the probabilities. Assuming we are willing to take the more complicated and reasonable route of trying to determine if it can be done right, two basic questions arise: Can it be done safely from a technical and economic standpoint? And second, if it can, will it be done accordingly? The first is a technical and economic matter; the second has to do with credibility.

Further consideration must be given to the unintended consequences of not allowing the project to go forward. From an environmental perspective, we must ask where will the oil go and under what conditions? From an economic perspective: How will we replace the jobs and business opportunities that we lose in stopping the project? From an over all sustainability perspective, the political (and geopolitical we might add) and social consequences might overshadow any possible environmental benefits of halting the project.

Since oil is not my area of expertise, let's consider a forestry-based example. We might ask ourselves what the over all effects of stopping timber production on our public forests, supposedly to save the Mexican Spotted Owl. We've lost a good part of our forest industry, meaning sustainable jobs. But also meaning that our forests are becoming overgrown, overstocked; just plain too thick, which also means that we are losing (in a human timeframe) significant areas of forest stands to fire. They will be replaced by Nature over time, but what happens to Spotted Owl habitat, not to mention the many other benefits of our forests? This is an example of unintended consequences of a "just say no" strategy. What has been the real agenda of those behind the Spotted Owl movement? It can be argued that it was to stop tree cutting. If so, this would be a case of a hidden agenda. If this is not the case, then why hasn't the approach been "lets try to find a way to make productive forest management compatible with wildlife habitat? This would have been the reasonable approach. In any case there is little doubt that the strategy was well intended but most likely misguided due to a lack of understanding of forest ecology and the dynamics of forest ecosystems.

We must understand that forest ecosystems are dynamic resilient entities and base our strategies accordingly.

A Taos News reader's response to this article ("Environmental decisions ...") led to writing our next item on matters related to dealing with corporations and environmental aspects of mineral and renewable natural resources management.

Corporations and Natural Resources

The Taos News – Natural Resources Notebook – Apr. 26 – May 2, 2012 - p. C2

What is or should be the role of corporations in dealing with natural resources?

Corporations, like globalization, are a fact of life. They exist and they are a power to deal with. Whether or not they can be trusted is another question.

What are corporations? Are they people? Apparently they are according to our Supreme Court, in so far as their ability to contribute to political campaigns. Does this mean that when they misbehave they can be put in jail like the rest of us? Actually, they are of course made up of people, from top executives, CEO's, to workers. Also they are made up of all who own shares, which include regular people with their mutual funds etc. and other large-scale investors from individuals to other corporations.

Another fact of life is that there are activities that, due to their complexity and need of large-scale finances, by nature have to be carried out by large organizations. Fossil energy, extraction, transport and refining demand large scale financing, engineering that can only be done by large entities: either corporations or state-owned companies (also corporations) such as those that exist in Mexico and Venezuela (PEMEX and PDVSA).

First of all, it would be wise to consider separately the matter of corporations (the "who" in management) from the technical, environmental and economic (the "how" part of management) elements of any proposed project in natural resources. Determining whether a proposed development such as the Keystone Pipeline, tar-oil sands or fracking can be done safely (for the environment) involves highly technical aspects, which must be considered and evaluated. The question of who is to go about doing it is another matter.

Regarding forest ecosystem resources, over all sustainability should be based on an optimum balance between extractive and non-extractive use. This involves land use planning based on multiple objectives ranging from material or energy production to a wide range of environmental services and aptitude of specific areas of forest based on stand, topography and soil characteristics. Sustainable productive forest management could include a possible forest energy initiative, as proposed in our last column. This would ideally involve establishing pilot-scale projects to further develop forest management practices in a multiple use framework that would also serve as demonstration areas for public education, wood industry, job training and possibly even rehab services, as well as environmental services.

Again, we should differentiate between sustainable productive forest management as an option from who should do it. How forests can be managed for production depends on the composition of the forests among other things. Forests composed largely of shade tolerant species such as our spruce and fir can be managed on selection systems with minimum alteration. In contrast, forests composed mostly of shade intolerants such as Douglas fir or aspen will be managed with more intensive practices, including clear-cutting. In fact even preserving shade-intolerant aspen forest stands over long periods of time involves some form of clear-cutting. If left alone, Nature will replace these stands with shade-tolerant spruce and fir.

Corporations no doubt are powerful entities. And the tendency is for them to become more and more powerful, both in economic and political terms (one leads to the other). How does society deal with them? Much of the answer lies in politics; but also regarding natural resources, in establishing checks and balances including multi-party monitoring.

Now all that remains to do in our adventure in ecology and forest management is wind up with an anniversary article that sums up the experience of the first three years of the Natural Resources Notebook column in the Taos News: 2007 – 2010.

WINDING UP OUR ADVENTURES IN ECOLOGY AND FOREST MANAGEMENT

The third anniversary of the Taos News Natural Resources Notebook is the last article in our journey of adventure. It includes historical notes of the column and some comments by the author.

Anniversary: Three years of the Natural Resources Notebook

The Taos News – Natural Resources Notebook. Oct 21 - 27, 2010. p. C11

The first article of The Taos News Natural Resources Notebook was published in the Oct 18 – 24, 2007 edition. The editor at that time was Gerald Garner who coined the name of the column and set up the bi-weekly routine. At first I had hoped that it would be a team endeavor but it soon developed into a one-person matter with the notable exception of UNM-Taos Geology Debbie Ragland's valuable editing and writing early on.

Around 78 articles make up the volume of my contribution to the Taos News. I have not received payment from any organization nor person for the column. It has been strictly a desire to share ideas, experiences and viewpoints with Taos News readers *aquí* en Taos and far beyond through the fine Internet access provided by the The Taos News. I have put most of my manuscripts on my website where the material is available at no cost. Searching the Internet with phrases and terms from the articles has shown that many are available on a range of information sites, some of which are pay-as-you-go. The column has reached a wide range of readers and the material is readily available for any interested in finding it on the Internet.

My agenda. I know, this doesn't sound good but I think everybody has some form of agenda. I believe that it's good and that it needs to be transparent and honest, meaning no hidden agenda in the actions that we take as citizens of our country and as citizens of the world. I feel that at present we are out of balance in our treatment, in our policies, regarding our forests. It seems that most people don't realize how dynamic and resilient our forest ecosystems are. This in no way implies that we shouldn't be careful, that we shouldn't operate on the precautionary principle. But all extremes are unhealthy, for people and for forests. Over-protecting can and will lead to more "loss" considered in human timescale. Forest ecosystems are never permanently lost or there just wouldn't be any left. This is thinking on a geologic time frame where a thousand years is a short period of time. Think of how many forest were lost in the ice ages, along with the soils scraped away by glaciers.

In the series we have covered a wide range of topics, from basic ecology concepts (What is ecology?) through more advance topics such as ecological succession and forest ecosystem resilience. Forest treatment has been addressed extensively in the Healthy Forest Buffer Zone series of articles, on through sustainability matters and monitoring, which involves, or should involve, the public in the form of multi-party monitoring, as part of balance and checks in our handling of forest resources. There have been articles on watersheds. We have ventured into the tropics with articles on tropical seasonal forests in Venezuela and Bolivia.

Renewable energy has been an important topic on the potential of forest biomass as an important part of our country's over all energy policies and strategies. This should be taken into consideration in the energy bill that's pretty much stalled in Congress right now.

I most sincerely thank the Taos News for the opportunity and readers for their comments and feedback. All information and opinions are my responsibility and do not reflect those of the Taos News or anyone else.

It is the author's most sincere wishes that our adventure has been fruitful and maybe even challenging, possibly regarding some postures assumed, which may have been controversial: like What's wrong with logging? I hope that readers will be motivated to continue the adventure and to use the experience for a productive role in helping society to better deal with our forest resources for the benefit of all forever.

EPILOGUE

In our adventurous journey through a quite wide range of topics, we have finally arrived at where we, meaning each of our readers who have had the patience and interest, probably, hopefully, have evolved in our thinking of how best to deal with forest ecosystems for the maximum benefit of human societies and for our planet Earth, forever.

The journey does not have an end. There will always be more questions that arise from our striving to find answers. Our knowledge of how forest ecosystems work and how they respond to events is on-going.

The author's hopes are that readers will pursue the various topics of interest and through the effort, become more well-informed activists, whether the action is just forming and expressing opinions or more direct involvement in planning, implementing and, especially, monitoring forest management. The author also intends to continue writing and sharing thoughts in the present context and approach for the benefit of the general public.

The adventure in ecology and forest management goes on.

APPENDIX A: TAOS NEWS NATURAL RESOURCES NOTEBOOK PUBLISHED ARTICLES

Appendix A

Date: July 4, 2012 File: Appendix A.xls

Year No.	Article - Published Title	Edition (Week)	P.
2007			
1	Global warming and forest health	Oct 18 - 24	B10,B11
2	Monitoring and Credibility	Nov 1 - 7	
3	What is ecology?	Nov 15 - 21	B11
4	Ethanol: If Brazil can, why can't we?	Nov 29 - Dec 5	C10
5	Save a tree, use a hand dryer instead	Dec 13 - 19	C10
6	Clear-cutting in the forest	Dec 27 - Jan 2	
2008			
7	Clear-cutting in the forest - Second in a 2-part series	Jan 3 - 9	
8	Preservation is sustainable if you accept change	Jan 10 - 16	
9	Global Dimming: An Inconvenient Complication?	Jan 24 - 30	
10	Our Environment: Protect it or Manage it?	Feb 7 - 13	B11
11	Forest management in Bolivia's subtropical seasonal forest	Feb 21 - 27	
12	Taking the earth's temperature a complicated process	Feb 28 - Mar 5	C10
13	What is an Ecosystem? Look around you"	Mar 20 - 26	

2010

APPENDIX B: SOME COMMENTS BY THE AUTHOR ON THE WRITING ADVENTURE

My objective in The Taos News Natural Resources Notebook is to stimulate thinking and awareness on basic ecological principles and the fact that forest ecosystems can be sustainably managed for production in combination with other uses such as water, recreation and biodiversity and soil conservation. This is my stated agenda. Often there is a difference between a stated agenda and a hidden agenda that is assumed for some purpose. As an example, in my view, it would appear that the whole matter around the spotted owl used to shut down forest industries in western US was (and is) an example of a hidden agenda. The open, stated, agenda was to save the spotted owl. The hidden agenda was to stop tree cutting, which has resulted in unintended consequences, namely greater loss of forests to insect, disease and, especially, wildfire. It seems that at present we are out of balance in our treatment and our policies regarding forests and that a majority of citizens don't realize how dynamic and resilient our forest ecosystems are. This in no way implies that we shouldn't be careful, that we shouldn't operate on the cautionary principle. But all extremes are unhealthy, for people and for forests. Over-protecting can and will lead to more "loss", where loss means within a human timescale. Forest ecosystems are never permanently lost or there just wouldn't be any left. This is thinking on a geologic time frame where a million years is a short period of time. Just think of how many forest were lost in the ice ages!

So, as the fourth anniversary of the Natural Resources Notebook came and went it seemed that it was a good time to consolidate the fairly extensive and sometimes intensive, also controversial, material covered. First of all, a most sincere appreciation and expression of gratitude for The Taos News editors, staff and owners for the continued support and for providing a platform for sharing ideas. Thank you all. I also would like to reiterate that all ideas and opinions expressed in the series of articles are my responsibility and in no way is it intended that they reflect those of The Taos News or the University of New Mexico-Taos. The objective from the start has been to share ideas and hopefully stimulate thinking and achieve a widening of viewpoints and open-mindedness of the general public. Great effort has been made to keep a balance between too scientific and too simple. It remains for the readers to decide to what degree that has been achieved.

At first the idea for the Natural Resources Notebook was to establish a writing group, mostly UNM-Taos. I greatly appreciate the contributions made by Dr. Debbie Ragland, UNM-Taos Geology, for her valuable time, editing and writing during the first stage. There came a time when keeping up with the writing send-in deadline for each issue did not allow time for such reviews.

For the curious, I might briefly describe my writing process. First of all, of course, it's all on word processor, namely MicroSoft Word®. e-mail has been the means by which I get the articles to the Editor from wherever I may be, often from as far away as Bolivia. The process for a given article starts with an idea that can come to mind at anytime and even in the strangest places (I won't go into detail on them) and times. I am known for carrying a pocket notebook all the time (Jenny, my mother, calls it my file cabinet and Maria, my wife, my *archivateca*). The ideas often come in Spanish as do the initial notes. Often a brief outline follows, on a page in one of the notebooks (the paper ones), sometimes not. So, often there is a paper trail and I do keep the notebooks, each labeled with dates and general prevailing location. The first organized step is starting to write on the computer and saving the seed idea with initial text in a folder titled "Initial Stage". I use both Mac® and PC with the necessary (over kill) backups all over the place. Whew, what a relief when USB port pen-drives (flash-drives) became more economically available! When the text gets near, or often beyond the now 570-character limit, it goes to the "Final Stage" folder; usually with a few days to let it cool off in order to catch the wilder ideas that find their way into the writing. That's one reason I prefer to write rather than speak. I get to really think over what comes out before I let it out! The final step is when the text file goes to the Ready Folder, in which there is a sub-folder Last Minute Corrections. Here the final draft is cut down to size, spell-checked by Word (thank you Mr. Bill Gates and team) and goes to the To Send to Editor folder. As a result each article has a history of development.

Writing is work but it's a lot of fun. I thank my parents Craig and Jenny Vincent; my San Cristobal School (through 8th grade - a two-room rural school); Taos (New Mexico, USA) Junior High (one year 9th grade, especially Mrs. Virgil Gutierrez and Mrs. Lupe Vaughn, the latter in Spanish); my Taos High School teachers, among them Mr. Bonifacio Fernandez, Mrs. Dolmith (please forgive me for a couple of bad pranks), Mr. Celestino (Colorado) Romero, Mr. Virgil Gutierrez (the math helped a lot in the thinking and analyzing process); and at CSU, Ft. Collins, Dr. Weber (physics) who really tried to teach us how to think and reason, my first quarter English composition teacher (I really wish I could remember her name) and many others. There were many more and as happens when one starts naming people, many are left out.

A major step in writing was when I decided that I had to learn to think and write directly on a typewriter (yes one of those old things, that we had along with a slide-rule, not even a calculator then in 1966). The writing step actually took place at The University of Tennessee, Knoxville while doing doctorate studies in 1975-76. Yes we had computers then but it was mostly punched cards for the IBM 370 that weren't much better than a typewriter (it's damn hard to fill in those little holes once punched on the cards that were fed into the huge machine). We never did really see the beast. Interactive DEC-10 was just coming in. No one that I knew thought of writing on a computer.

So, when in 1981 I happened to see an Apple II+ computer in a store in Merida, Venezuela, I bought it. Shortly after, once I had a 51/4 inch floppy drive (and those really were floppy), I somehow discovered word processing and bought an Apple word processor (What was it called, Applewriter?). My printer was an Apple silent-type that printed on thermal paper. You could barely read it but my Universidad de Los Andes (ULA) forestry students didn't have any alternative. At one time the forestry college Faculty Council discussed and approved the idea of masters' theses being written on a computer.

The word was in the school: "Why would Larry use a computer to write with?"

Now, many years later, the writing adventure continues. I hope that we can all enjoy it, both on the writing end and the reading. To all my readers: my thanks in advance to you for your interest and hopefully for your feedback in some form.

APPENDIX C: FOREST BIOPOWER

Adventures in ecology and forest management is brought to you by Forest BioPower. This book is part of a strategy and over all effort to promote open-minded thinking regarding what to do with public and private forests all over the world.

Forest BioPower is a company based on forest ecosystem science and human needs and on the idea that a sustainable balance between productive forest management and preservation is the best approach to achieve maximum benefits for society and the environment.

The goal of Forest BioPower is to explore and promote the huge potential of vast forest ecosystems in renewable energy, economic development and climate change mitigation. Exploring involves thinking; the development of ideas involving sharing ideas, taking them apart and putting them back together in a multi-party effort based on a systems analysis approach. Promoting the ideas involves public outreach, education, information distribution through all possible media.

Interested parties, whether individuals or organizations can get involved through the Forest BioPower Network, where information, ideas, projects, proposals are available to members in an interactive environment. Members can participate in the Forest BioPower Blog, have access to the Forest BioPower Notebook, Forest BioPower Document Center and take part in Forest BioPower Education.

The reader is invited to visit Forest BioPower at:

www.forestbiopower.com

www.silvibiopower.com

www.forestbiopower.com.ve

www.cmb-lwv.com.ve

Made in the USA
Monee, IL
07 July 2026

56552150R00125